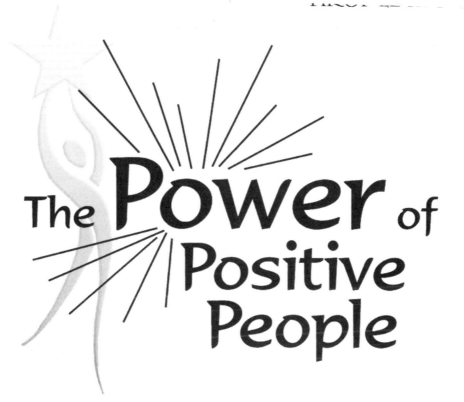

# The Power of Positive People

*You can turn to any page*
*and find the very thought*
*or the very connection to enrich your life*
*in the next day or the next moment of your journey.*
*Keep it close at hand. Refer to it often.*
*Share it with those you love.*

New Light Publishing Company
Gaithersburg, Maryland

Copyright 2004 New Light Publishing / Pat Sampson
267 Kentlands Boulevard, Gaithersburg, Maryland 20878
newlightstars@aol.com
www.newlightstars.com


ISBN 0-9749159-0-4


Library of Congress Cataloging in Publication data available through the Library of Congress.


Publisher:  New Light Publishing / Pat Sampson
Book Layout:  Doug Hyde and Brian Holscher
Cover Designer and Book Illustrator:  Susan Emily Pitt

# Dedication

*To all who were my teachers*
*...and still are.*

To my two beautiful daughters,
and two wonderful grandsons,
a source of great inspiration and pride,
whose faith in me never wavered
and whose encouragement inspired me
to continue reaching for the stars

To friends who believed in this dream
and my ability to make it happen.
I have lost touch with some of you
and hope you will contact me.

To all positive people who know that
to be who you are and to become
all that you are capable of becoming,
is a journey of discovery leading to
happiness and success.

# Acknowledgements

My deepest appreciation to all contributors
and sponsors who in a spirit of love and giving
shared their life experiences and philosophies
to enhance the lives of others.

Doug Hyde and Brian Holscher for all their hard work
to produce a book worthy of our contributors
and readers and for "Every Man"
evaluations and suggestions.

Sean Hill for his valued input and understanding.

Deborah Eby for editing;
Katherine Rabenau for proofreading.

Susan Emily Pitt, a miracle
who arrived via cyberspace on Christmas Day
from across the world in Africa
at a time when I most needed her friendship
and her wealth of talents
to edit, to counsel, to illustrate and to create a
magnificent cover and website.

Expect a Miracle!

# A Journey of Discovery

### how thought shapes your destiny

Dear Friends ~

One of the greatest lessons of my lifetime was gleaned from the pages of the classic: *Think and Grow Rich*. I learned that a *strong positive attitude works powerfully in anything you set out to do and in any circumstance in which you find yourself.* This perception changed my life, liberating me from the illusion that we are victims of our circumstances and awoke a sense of wonder, joy and the inspiration that what your thoughts are, you become. This kind of thinking became my life-line and the basis of an extremely successful sales career which was later set aside to follow what many called a most unrealistic journey.

I dreamed of creating a venue for contemporary positive people to share their life experiences ~ the joys and the pain, the challenges, and the glitter of achievement; the triumph of hope over reality; and the resilience of the spirit in bringing about results beyond the realm of human understanding. It is true that by keeping the faith you find resources at your command that you never dreamt possible. Willingness to foster a positive attitude in any given set of circumstances is to consciously and deliberately choose one's way. This power of will and belief in one's own inner resources springs from faith, commitment and a strong desire to lead a meaningful and fulfilling life of true discovery.

The people you meet within these pages represent all walks of life. Some are famous authors, business or spiritual leaders, while other extraordinary people you may be meeting for the first time. All have a wonderful philosophy of hope and optimism. You will find positive visions to inspire and motivate you, as well as winning strategies and practical exercises encouraging you to live your dream and continue reaching for the stars!

I would love to hear from you.

Pat Sampson, Publisher
newlightstars@aol.com

# New Light Stars

## IN ALPHABETICAL ORDER

You are capable
of anything and everything.
You set goals and reach them
You dream dreams and make them come true.
You are no less a miracle than the seas you sail
and the skies under which you live.
You know you can have everything in life you desire
If you will just help other people realize their dreams.

You follow the light of your own individuality.
Always learning, accepting the new, anticipating the best.
Believing whether life is beautiful or adverse ~
that it has meaning and purpose.
You handle the challenges life sends your way.
Knowing that each lesson ~ no matter how difficult
is an opportunity to learn and grow.

You are here to be happy; to be fulfilled; to be joyful.
You have this amazing power to be the You
that you are really meant to be,
and create the life you've always yearned for.
You become energized, inspired and stimulated,
by finding and connecting with kindred spirits,
who dare to fulfill their dreams and
reach for the stars!

# Contents

# A CREED
## for positive people

We greet each day with an optimistic attitude.
We speak of hope and prosperity.
We see everyone including ourselves as
   worthwhile and deserving.
We acknowledge that the most
   important thing is growth in comparison
   only to oneself, not in comparison to others.
We avoid the plague of pessimists.
We know that the worst bankruptcy
   is a loss of enthusiasm.
We forget the mistakes of the past
   yet grow by the lessons they teach.
We surround ourselves with people
   who are productive and inspired.
We go where good words are spoken.
We are unafraid of questioning old beliefs
   in the light of new evidence.
We are able to change.
We honor Mother Earth
We believe in a loving Higher Power.
We take pleasure in our diversity.
We exercise our own religious beliefs,
   political and personal  preferences
   and do not infringe on the rights of others
   to do the same.
We are positive role models.
We know that to have a friend, you first must be one.
We appreciate others and tell them so.
We support each other's aspirations as we support our own.

## Together we light the way
### to a brighter tomorrow!

www.newlightstars.com

# TODAY

Today I begin my life anew,
Whether the sky holds a brilliant sun
Or pours refreshing rain.
I feel energized, ready
To create the life I desire.

Today I project
What I want to experience
Who I am and who I become
Is always mine to decide.

I commit myself to the expression
Of my endless possibilities.
Living on this beautiful and bountiful planet,
I cherish the riches of ideas flooding my mind,
The health flowing through my body,
And my sensitivity to the beauty of life ~
May I never grow numb to it.

As my understanding and awareness grows
I accept everything I do
As the result of choice
And I surrender into the light
Of self acceptance and more love,
And release all negative beliefs that
Rob me of my joy and power.
I free myself from guilt and fear.

What I desire controls me,
So I nurture new ideas and new ways of thinking
To attract more and more openness.
And a sense of oneness
With every other human being.
There are no strangers in my life,
Only friends I haven't met.

If any wait to discourage me,
I will go on my way,
For the greatest help I can be
Is to live a positive life,
Inspiring others to do the same.

# TERRY COLE-WHITTAKER, Ph.D

World renowned inspiring and motivating speaker, best-selling author, television minister and producer, business consultant, & counselor to the "stars" **Terry Cole-Whittaker** is a catalyst for enlightenment, bliss, love, and prosperity.

Her television ministry is legendary. Her foundation has built the International Library and Institute for Sacred Knowledge in Asia. Dr. Cole-Whittaker ministers to a global congregation through her foundation's internet outreach and travels the world teaching the "Principles of Successful Living."

Her students and clients are the "Who's Who" of global leaders, artists, spiritual and business leaders. She is the best-selling author of *What You Think of Me is None of My Business*, and the New York Times # 1 *How to Have More in a Have Not World, and Dare to Be Great.* She was inducted into the Hall of Fame of her college. Three times she was voted as Headliner of the Year by San Diego Press, and has received three honorary doctorate degrees for her spiritual work.

Dr. Terry has been featured on over 800 TV programs, been featured in the most important magazines and newspapers in the world. In the best-selling book, *10 Women of Power*, she is listed as one of the 10 most powerful and inspirational women in the world.

**Rev. Terry Cole-Whittaker can be reached at www.terrycolewhittaker.com or info@terrycolewhittaker.com**

Do not fear no matter the appearances, but keep on your spiritual path and endeavor to build your consciousness and bring forth the greatness that is within you. The only hope of the world is that individuals know who they are, accept the abundance and love of God, and express this love in everything they think, feel, and do. We do this by reaching beyond where we are and by accepting the challenge of manifesting our divine potential.

## Impossible Goals Can Be Attained

Why not set goals that look almost impossible to attain? Many teachers advise their students to set realistic goals, but those teachers are not aware of the supernatural laws of the universe or the divine purpose of life.

Realistic goals keep us playing small, safe, and unchallenged. Because a goal that is unrealistic is so impossible, we must depend upon God to help us to achieve it. And to do this we must reach way beyond where we are and grow spiritually, mentally and emotionally.

Most people seek comfort or to just get by and make ends meet, but it is the rare soul, who seeks to attain the topmost that is possible for any human being. This is actually what is required if we want to gain entrance and access to bliss, opulence, and glory of God's kingdom in the here and now.

Every person is destined for greatness. Greatness means maximizing one's options and developing oneself into the full expression of what they are, as a person with godlike qualities.

## Love is God

Obviously I am not just talking about the pursuit of material things alone, as this kind of goal only leads to failure. There is not enough stuff in the universe to satisfy the person who is seeking to get love, happiness, peace of mind, and security from material things. Yet everyone needs material things to survive and flourish. The body is material and it needs material things, but the soul is spirit and it needs spirit to thrive. Love is God, and it is the love we seek.

For most their mission is to make enough money to pay the rent or mortgage, buy the groceries, pay the bills, and find relief from their mental, emotional, and physical problems. Unfortunately this kind of a material mission alone without a higher purpose and mission produces only stress, distress, and dissatisfaction and keeps a person slave to his or her fears. With the emphasis on material energy we are stuck in lack and limitation, seeing only what we do not have. Material things come to us naturally when we are engrossed and engaged in doing our mission and life's work.

## Discovering and Doing Your Life's Work

The goal of life is not food, clothing, and shelter, and yet of course these are necessary so that we can do our life's work. The body is a vehicle and a temple through which we can worship and serve Spirit. The body has needs so that we can perform our mission and purpose, which is spiritual. When we serve Spirit and others, with love all our needs are met. Focusing on matter and things, which are secondary, makes us lose sight of the primary objective: love of God and others. Love means to give, to empower, to serve, to enrich, to make happy and to prosper.

## Spiritual Solutions to Material Problems

There are solutions to our material problems, but these solutions are spiritual and not material. Spirit is senior to matter. When we are aware of our godlike spiritual nature, the supernatural powers of God, and the laws of universe, we really can have it all including both spiritual and material riches.

What I am talking about are the benefits one receives from living a spiritually motivated life. A spiritually motivated life is one in which the person has a purpose greater than themselves, a mission to be of service and to reach the goal of life, God and self-realization. This kind of a purpose brings the greatest possible of all benefits. What people are missing is a personal relationship with God and a mission that is worthy of the person.

We need to be challenged to both bring forth the greatness that is within us and to trust in a Higher Supernatural Power and Presence to work with us in manifesting our dreams and goals into reality all for the greater good of the all.

## Dream Your Dream

No one with a great dream and vision, who works to attain them, has ever gone without whatever they need both spiritually and materially. A sad soul is one who identifies themselves as the body and has forgotten that they are an eternal soul, made in the image and likeness of God. This person lives in fear of death, and is threatened constantly by the ever-changing world around them. Never give up your dream because others are trying to frighten you, but be courageous and even more determined. Remember that success is the best revenge.

Jesus told us to "Live in this world, but not of it." We are not of this world, but we are traveling through it. An enlightened soul never believes in the appearances of this world, but believes in who they are, the value of his or her mission, and the eternal and ever-present power presence of God. They will believe they will succeed and prosper in their mission and endeavors, regardless of outer appearances or world conditions.

## Be Extra-ordinary

Extraordinary people are ordinary people who do extraordinary things. Blessings come through us, as we must have the consciousness for whatever it is we want to experience and attain. Whatever is our heart's desire, it is we who must become the vehicle through which that desire can be made manifest. It may be challenging to think of what is really available to us, as we may think, "How could I ever attain that or do that?"

Remember, whatever any person has attained, is attaining, or will attain is possible for you and every other person to attain. The only way we will have faith in the Supreme and be able to taste the Divine is to think big and be willing to be used, as a tool of the divine to do great works.

## THE THREE KEYS TO FORTUNE.

Once you set your sights on a goal far beyond where you are, you set the universal creative machine in motion. Within time, which is only as long as it takes for you to believe and accept it as already yours, it *must* manifest. This is the law of life. The mystical power of Divine Intelligence moves on our ideas and desires and works everything out in the right way, and at the right time, and beyond our understanding. We don't make it work. We use it. Everyone is using this mystical power in every moment, *whether they know it or not.* Follow the instructions *exactly* to get the results you want. Do not be fooled into thinking that, because these keys are very simple, they are not profound and powerful. They are *very* profound, and *very* powerful.

# The First Key
### *Write a list of your desires.*

You must know what it is you desire to manifest. Writing your desires, as to what you would like to be, do, and have, is the beginning, and most important, step in the creative process. Choose greatness of self to develop your divine potential. Take the limitations off your thinking and imagine your possibilities. What would you like to *be?*

### Write down your *being* desires.

1. _____

2. _____

3. _____

4. _____

5. _____

6. _____

7. _____

## Write down your *doing* desires.

1. _____

2. _____

3. _____

4. _____

5. _____

6. _____

7. _____

## Write down your *having* desires

1. _____

2. _____

3. _____

4. _____

5. _____

6. _____

7. _____

*"Every great soul throughout history was a person like you and me ~ a simple soul. You have a mission in your heart and it is for you alone to fulfill it. Do it now! Greatness is your destiny!"*

# The Second Key

### *Read your list of desires once a day*

Sometime during the day, preferably first thing in the morning or the last thing at night, work with your list. Read the list, removing any desires that you realize aren't that important or worthwhile, and add others that are. If you want faster results, do this two times a day, once in the morning and also right before you go to sleep.

While reading each item on your list do two more things: *Imagine that each item has already been given to you,* and feel as you would if you had received and achieved each goal and desire. By guiding and directing Divine Energy, which is forever flowing through your mind, with words, thoughts, and emotions that are beneficial, positive, empowering, and specific, you are blessing yourself and using the creative law of life as it was meant to be used.

See yourself as the person you desire to *be*, doing what you desire to be *doing*, and *having* what you would like to have. Whatever you would like to have happen, have it happen within the creative studio of your mind first. Within time it will appear in the outer world. Time is relative. Manifestation of your desire appears in the instant you can *accept* whatever it is you desire to mentally, emotionally, and physically manifest.

Believing means to walk, talk, think, speak, and act as the person you now know that you are. Believe in the power of God to heal *in an instant* and you are that healing channel through which God's healing energy is flowing. If you choose to limit yourself by disbelieving, you will limit yourself. Otherwise, the rich resources, intelligence, power, love, peace and bliss of the Universe are yours to use for your every good and wonderful purpose.

# The Third Key

*Have faith and believe, beyond a shadow of a doubt.*

There is something very special about this prayer: *It works all the time, without fail, if the person believes.* And so, after you work with your lists, speak this prayer with feeling *every day:*

---

*I am a rich child of a loving and wealthy Divine Father. Divine Intelligence is now showing me what I need to do to claim that which I desire. Divine Intelligence is even now opening the doors to my immediate blessings in ways beyond my understanding.*

*Money, love, and opportunities for my immediate and long-term good fortune, are flowing into, around, and through me now. I receive and accept my good. What I desire also desires me, and is now being irresistibly drawn into my experience. My word must be fulfilled, as this is the law of divine creativity. I have absolute faith that all that is mine by Divine Right now comes to me in rich abundance.*

*As I speak my word and decree a thing, it is done in Divine Right order and right on time. God is my Source and my true supply. Universal Intelligence is responding to the claim I am making, and is manifesting my desire into form, as I speak. This is certain, I am certain, and my faith is absolute.*

*It is done, and I say: "Thank You, God, and so it is."*

---

After speaking your prayer with faith and confidence, release it into God's hands and go about your work knowing for certain that, in the right time and in the right way, you will receive every item on your list. . . or something far better.

# Dr. Benjamin S. Carson Sr., M.D.

Photo by Keith Weller

**Benjamin S. Carson, Sr., M.D.** is director of pediatric neurosurgery at the Johns Hopkins Medical Institutions, a position he has held since 1984.

Dr. Carson is the recipient of numerous honors and awards, including 22 honorary doctorate degrees, and is named in the book *Who's Who in America*. He is a member of the Horatio Alger Society of Distinguished Americans, the American Academy of Achievement, and the Alphas Omega Alpha Medical Honor Society, among others. He is also a Fellow of the Yale Corporation, the governing body of Yale University.

Dr. Carson addresses groups of school children, urging them to use their intellectual potential to achieve success in life. His autobiography, *Gifted Hands*, chronicles the road from dire poverty, poor self-esteem, and horrible grades to his life as an adult. Subsequent books, *Think Big* and *Getting the Big Picture*, elaborate on his work as a surgeon and his philosophy for success in life. He is president and founder of the Carson Scholars Fund, which encourages academic excellence in young Americans of all backgrounds.

Dr. Benjamin Carson is married and has three sons.

# Ghetto Kid To...

## World Renowned
## Pediatric Neurosurgeon

**Excerpts from Publisher's Interview with the famous and inspiring Dr. Benjamin S. Carson, Sr., M.D**

B*enjamin Carson was raised in the squalid surroundings of one of Detroit's toughest, poorest neighborhoods, in a cramped tumbled-down tenement, next to railroad tracks. Filled with rage against an absent father, Ben and his brother, Curtis, experienced the hopelessness and despair felt by many inner-city children.*

---

*"Dr. Carson works miracles on children others have written off as hopeless".*
Barbara Walters, ABC News, "20-20".

---

Very few mothers had as rough a time as mine. Because she didn't have an education, she worked ten to fifteen hours a day as a domestic, trying to keep us off welfare. *"Do your best and God will take care of the rest,"* she'd say over and over. Even though she was one of 24 children and got married at 13 and found out her husband was a bigamist and only had a 3rd grade education and had to work menial jobs, she was not a victim. I think one of the best things she ever did for my brother and myself was to disabuse us from the victims' mentality. Daily she drummed into Curtis and me that we had to do our best in school. She would never accept excuses. She would always say, *"Do you have a brain? Then you can do something."* But I was anything but a good student. But my mother never gave up on me. *"You weren't born to be a failure, Bennie,"* she'd say. *"You can be anything you want to be."* Sometimes, I'd get tired of hearing it. I wished she would just accept the fact that I was the class dummy. Everybody else knew it. But she wouldn't give up, insisting I read two books a week. *"Reading is the way out of ignorance,"* she'd insist. My mother was right. I found out how right, in the fifth grade.

One day, our science teacher held up a piece of black glass-like rock. *"Does any-body know what this is? And what does it have to do with volcanoes?"* I played with rocks around the railroad tracks and at mother's insistence, read about them. Immediately, I recognized the stone. I couldn't believe none of the smart kids raised their hand. When I raised mine, the jeering threatened to disturb order. *"Obsidian,"* I said, over the laughter. *"And it's formed by the super-cooling of lava when it hits water."* *"That's right,"* the teacher said, startled. *"Wow, look at them,"* I recall thinking, *"they're looking at me with admiration."* It felt like it must feel to win the million-dollar lottery. At that moment, my perspective changed. I knew the ability to change my life was within me; it wasn't some external force. I had control. I didn't want to be the class dummy anymore. I started reading everything I could find. Biographies of astronauts, surgeons, oceanographers. Within a year, I zoomed to the top of the class.

*We are not victims of our circumstances. We can change them if we believe we can. But the problem with the younger generation today is that they are buying into what the media feeds them.*

*We are not victims of our circumstances.* We can change them if we believe we can. But the problem with the younger generation today is that they are buying into what the media feeds them. This creates a sense of hopelessness. They feel left out. Disempowered. Then, in order to "belong", they give in to peer pressure. I know, because it happened to me.

From the seventh to the tenth grade, I had a major, major problem. I wanted to be one of the guys. The ones who wore Italian knit shirts and stayed out late with the *"in"* crowd. Oh, I was getting *"high-fives"* and *"low-fives"*; and pats on the back. And that's all I cared about. My grades plummeted down the tubes; and the worst part was I didn't care. But at a deeper level I knew I was doing wrong.

I developed a pathological temper. I was easy to offend and I felt I had to inflict pain on the offender with a brick, a bottle, a knife, or anything else I could get my hands on. I was a good kid when I wasn't mad; but I was frequently mad. One day I became enraged at my best friend. I lunged at him with a knife. He was wearing a large metal belt buckle and my knife broke on it; or it would be a different story today. Horrified, I ran home and locked myself in the bathroom. I sat there shaking. I thought about my dreams to be a doctor. I thought about the stories I heard in church about the missionary doctors; to me, the noblest people in the world. At great personal sacrifice they went off to foreign lands to bring not only physical, but also mental and spiritual help to people. What could be more wonderful? And here I am almost killing my best friend.

> *Kids don't see role models who achieve intellectually elevated the same way that rock-stars and athletes are; so even though I don't like the limelight, I see it as a way to make a point. I speak at schools as much as my schedule permits. I try to inspire them to use the power of their mind as the way out of the ghetto.*

I prayed for three hours. I asked the Lord to take my temper away. I picked up the Bible that my mother kept in the bathroom and opened it up to the passage: *Proverb 14, Verse 29: He that is slow to wrath is of great understanding; but he that is hasty of spirit exalteth folly,' and Proverb 25: 28: He that hath no rule over his own spirit is like a city that is broken down and without walls.* I felt that these verses were written for me. When I left the bathroom, my temper was gone. And it never returned. I have never even needed to suppress it. God had taken it away. People who know me now can never even believe that I had a temper problem.

After that, I returned to school, and channeled all of my energy into my education. I knew the learning I needed as the way out of the ghetto went way beyond what was presented in the inner-city school curriculum. So after classes, I walked to the University and spent hours in the library. I went to art galleries, free concerts, museums; anything to expand my mind. Oh, the guys jeered at me and called me names. But none of it fazed me. I'd say, "Let's see where you are in twenty years, and see where I am." Some of that *"in"* crowd are *"in"* for life.

Kids don't see role models who achieve intellectually elevated the same way that rock-stars and athletes are; so even though I don't like the limelight, I see it as a way to make a point. I speak at schools as much as my schedule permits. I try to inspire them to use the power of their mind as the way out of the ghetto. What if they knew as they were growing up that, let's say they were taking a walk down a street that it was Charles Brooks, a black man, who invented the street sweeper. Or down the street comes one of those big refrigerator tractor-trailers and you pointed out to them that it was Frederick Jones, a black man, who invented the refrigeration system for trucks. And it stops at the red light and you tell them it was Garrett Morgan, a black man, who invented the traffic signal. You tell how he also invented the gas mask.

And while you're talking about war, you're talking about Henrietta Bradbury, a black woman, who invented the underwater cannon and made it possible to launch torpedoes from submarines. And as you walk past a hospital you will talk about Charles Drew and his understanding of blood plasma and blood transfusions. You will talk about Daniel Helm Williams, the first successful open heart surgeon. You will also talk about Lewis Latimer when you look up at the lights and how he did pioneering work in incandescent and fluorescent lighting and invented the electric lamp diagram that was helpful for Alexander Graham Bell.

You go across the railroad tracks. Andrew Beard, the Jenny-automatic railroad car coupler. Elijah McCoy, the automatic lubrication system. In fact, he had so many inventions, when something new would come out people would say, "Is that a McCoy? Is that the *real McCoy?*" That's where the term comes from. You've got racist people talking about the real McCoy and don't even know who they're paying homage to.

But, you know, who'd have thought – what if these guys and gals knew that their ancestry had contributed all kinds of things to the development of this country, not just bouncing basketballs, and not just rapping? You know, maybe they might think of themselves in a little different light.

But a greater message is that you can take that same walk down the street for virtually any ethnic group in the United States and point out tremendous contributions that were made. That's how we got to be the pinnacle nation faster than any other nation in the history of the world, because we had so many people from so many backgrounds with so much talent. And what if we, as a people, learn how to harness that? What if we learn to be positive about that? What if we learn that being different is not a problem, it's a blessing.

I remind young people of the power of their own dream to make a difference. And then, I repeat the words my mother ingrained in me, growing up:

*"As long as you are satisfied that you have done your best, then that is all you have to do. Clothing is not important. Houses, cars and bank accounts. None of these are important. You know what is important? Knowledge and hard work. Those abilities allow you to acquire those things and to have pride in yourself. You know what is important? Here is how you figure it out. Just let someone take all the things away from you; like money, cars and houses. You can get them back if you have the knowledge and learn how to use it. But if someone takes away your knowledge, and your willingness to give your best, you've lost everything that is important."*

Besides my mother, I owe everything to God. That, and the determination that through knowledge and the pursuit of excellence, I could reach my dreams if I would

## Think **BIG!**

# THINK

**T** *is for talent.* God has provided each of us with certain specific talents and we should strive to recognize these and to develop them. Once these talents are highly developed, they can be used in one's career choice. Obviously, if one chooses a career in which he or she has significant talent, that individual will already have a head start on others choosing that career.

**H** *is for honesty.* If one is honest in all one's words and deeds, one does not need to concern one's self about what was said or done in the past.

This uncomplicates the life significantly and allows one to concentrate on the task at hand.

**I** *is for insight.* Insight is gained by listening to people who have already gone down the path that you are seeking to travel. There is absolutely no reason that you should repeat the same mistake that others made and there is every reason to gain from their mistakes. Insight is also gained by reading uplifting materials with broad perspectives on world events and historical events. The *Bible* is a good example.

**N** *is for nice.* It is much easier to be nice to people than to hold grudges and be unkind. Also, if you are nice to people, generally speaking, in the long run they will be nice to you. Remember, the people you meet on the way up are the same ones you meet on the way down.

**K** *is for knowledge.* Knowledge unlocks the doors of opportunity and once you have it, it is difficult for anyone to deprive you of it.

# BIG!

**B** *is for books.* The learning that is derived from books is generally much more substantial than that derived from television. Book learning requires active participation of the mental processes at a much higher level than does television gazing. The constant mental activity obviously builds the mind in much the same way that physical activity builds muscles.

**I** *is for indepth learning.* This is to be compared with superficial learning. Superficial learning is done by people who like to cram material in before an exam, or who learn facts simply to impress others and then rapidly forget them. Indepth learning occurs when one actually wants to understand concepts and principles and wants to acquire knowledge for the sake of knowledge itself. This type of learning tends to stay with the individual and allows the individual to build upon it and become an independent and innovative thinker.

**G** *is for God.* It is important to realize that God is a real entity, capable of doing anything and providing those who accept him with an incredible advantage. I dare say that any person who decides to "THINK BIG" will be successful in any endeavor.

© Benjamin S. Carson, Sr., M.D.

# JACQUELINE DANFORTH

**Jacqueline Danforth** is the Executive Director of New Horizons Wilderness Program for young women in the State of Maine. Though she grew up in New York City, Jackie Danforth has always been a "nature girl" at heart. She brings a wealth of experience to her position as Executive Director, having worked in both medical and marketing fields. She is a graduate of an Alternative Therapeutic School, where she served as Vice President.

Jackie is married to Mark Danforth, a Maine native and Registered Maine Guide.

Visit our website, *http://www.daughtersatrisk.com*

*Send for our brochure or feel free to call our office with questions.*
New Horizons  P.O.Box 186    Orrington, Maine 04474
(207) 992-2424                info@daughtersatrisk.com

We hope you'll give us the privilege of introducing your daughter to one of the greatest places on earth.

New Horizons
WILDERNESS PROGRAM
*for young women*

**As Seen On:**
*Dateline NBC ~ Good Housekeeping ~
Ladies Home Journal ~ The View*

# Self-Discovery

*"Friendship with one's self is all important,
because without it one cannot be friends
with anyone else in the world."*
~ **Eleanor Roosevelt**


I am 34 years old, I grew up in New York City, was an "at risk teen," attended an alternative school out west, came back east after graduating high school and decided to open a program that was therapeutic nature based.

I had been living in Maine for a year when I decided to open Daughters, Inc. d.b.a. *New Horizons Wilderness Program* for young women. You could say I had an epiphany.

I am no one particularly special, I don't have any big degrees and I have held jobs ranging from cosmetic representative to veterinary assistant…. And OH YES, I do have a famous mom. But besides that I am very much a woman who wears the most comfortable clothes she can, I tell the truth (no matter how much trouble I get into…. And sometimes it's a lot! My mother says I don't have an unspoken thought). I try very hard every day to be a really good person ~ and I really love life and people! I am what you would call a scholar of not sociology, but humanology (if there is such a thing.) My favorite subjects are women and self discovery.

Let's see…. What is *self- discovery?* Let's look at these two words: *self* (meaning you) and *discovery* (notice it isn't discovered). The word *discovery* has no time limit placed on it. It is a life-long process that takes different forms in many different ways at all different times in our lives. I believe that society has an unspoken time frame of when *discovery* is supposed to be discovered.. . . in your late 20's through the 30's. I feel that society has changed and it is even harder these days to know who you are and how to honor that person.

*"This is your life~*
*not someone else's.*
*It is your own feeling of what is important,*
*not what people will say. Sooner or later, you are*
*bound to discover that you cannot please all of the*
*people around you all of the time. Some of them*
*will attribute to you motives you never dreamed of.*
*Some of them will misinterpret your words and*
*actions, making them completely alien to you. So*
*you had better learn fairly early that you must not*
*expect to have everyone understand what you say*
*and what you do. The important thing is to be sure*
*that those who love you, whether family or friends,*
*understand as nearly as you can make them*
*understand. If they believe in you, they will trust your*
*motives. But do not ask or expect to have anyone*
*with you on everything. Do not try for it. To reach*
*such a state of unanimity would mean that you*
*would risk losing your own individuality to attain it."*

**~ Eleanor Roosevelt**

I have been asking *"Who am I"* for years! I've found it varies from day to day, mood to mood, and even state to state:

The New York Answer: *"I am the owner and founder of New Horizons Wilderness Program for young women in the beautiful State of Maine."*

The LA Answer: *"I am a spiritual woman, a vegetarian and I recycle!"*

The Maine Answer: *"I am German/English so I am probably related to Paul, you know Paul ~ the snowplower and psychologist? Well his cousin Sue came from Germany and ~ and so on."*

So, you really need to define what self discovery really means. Is it tangible? Is it emotional? Is it spiritual? Or is it a little bit of everything wrapped up into the definition of *you*? For each one of us the definition is different. A person who feels emotionally secure might say that he/she knows who they are. Someone else who feels self-discovery comes from the job you hold may disagree and judge you by the career *they* hold.

The *big question is "What is the goal of life?"* I believe the answer lies in acceptance. In my line of work the biggest gift my company can teach teenage girls is to accept each other and to communicate in a non-judgmental way. This is obviously easier said than done. But it's not impossible. We need to realize as a society that we all are trying to find out who we are and how to honor that person. And it's not an easy task. But that's life. If we all work together to accept the truth ~ it may take a whole lifetime to know who you are ~ or you may never be able to answer that question ~ and this makes you a seeker, not a bad person. It will make others feel better if you are honest about it.

It's amazing how many people give a sigh of relief when you share with them the truth about yourself ~ both the good and the bad. The secret to human life is that everyone ~ and I mean *everyone* ~ wants to be accepted. I believe that when we as a society understand this secret and accept each other ~ scars and all ~ then and only then will we be honoring ourselves.

*Acceptance* is a very powerful secret…. Pass it along.

## MISSION STATEMENT

**At New Horizons, our mission is straight-forward, yet meaningful:**

*To inspire adolescent females – using the combined resources of the natural environment, caring, knowledgeable professionals, and the power of self-discovery – to enhance their individual mental, physical, social and spiritual well-being.*

**To inspire . . .**

The word "inspire" means to breathe into. Our job and privilege at New Horizons is to give your daughter the "fresh air" she needs – both literally and figuratively – to think, reflect, learn new skills, and ultimately, to make better choices.

**. . . adolescent females . . .**

Young women today are faced with very specific pressures and issues that are in many ways unprecedented. By specializing exclusively in teenage females, we believe we're able to provide a higher level of dedication, focus and effectiveness.

**. . . using the combined resources of the natural surroundings . . .**

Our northern Maine setting is among the most beautiful and unspoiled in the U.S. Through safe, nature-based activities such as canoeing, kayaking, hiking, camping and cross-country skiing, New Horizons provides an opportunity year-round for your daughter to experience the exhilarating, yet healing power of nature.

**. . . caring, knowledgeable professionals . . .**

A great staff is the lifeblood of any successful program. At New Horizons, ours is world-class. By hiring professionals with both a head and a heart for nurturing young women, we're able to provide an uncommonly effective level of intervention.

**. . . and the power of self-discovery . . .**

By taking part in a carefully designed and individualized, therapeutic plan your daughter will have the time, space, and focused attention she needs not only to realize the consequences of her negative choices and emotions, but also to remember her hopes and dreams and reaffirm her strengths.

**. . . to enhance their individual mental, physical, social and spiritual well being.**

At New Horizons, we take a caring, holistic, family-oriented approach. Our goal is to return your daughter to you more mentally focused; physically strengthened; socially responsible; and spiritually refreshed.

# THE STEPPINGSTONES OF GROWTH

*New Horizons' Team of Directors has developed a powerful emotional growth process to help your daughter build her confidence and self-esteem from better communication skills, and act responsibly toward herself and others. Here are our goals for her emotional growth while she's with us at New Horizons.*

**Truth**
*We will help your daughter to . . .*
Examine the excuses and lies she has created for herself
Share her personal story
Face her negative self-image
Learn how to communicate her emotions positively and effectively

**Friendship**
*We will help your daughter to . . .*
Learn the qualities of a healthy relationship
Discover how to give and receive guidance and set boundaries
Gain a sense of accountability and self-worth
Establish more positive social behaviors and attitudes

**Forgiveness**
*We will help your daughter to . . .*
Take responsibility for and understand any unhealthy choices
   she has made
Learn to stop playing the "blame-game"
Accept that parents are human too
Discover how to turn past failure into practical wisdom

**Acceptance**
*We will help your daughter to . . .*
Stop negative, self-destructive ways of thinking
Discover how to connect with her femininity and power
Establish a new, positive connection with family
Understand and accept both her strengths and weaknesses

**Passage**
*We will help your daughter to . . .*
Plan how she will begin to use her strengths in a healthy
   manner
Formulate a strategy for overcoming with setbacks
Learn skills on how to cope with the upcoming challenges she
   will be facing
Take the steps needed to transition into a responsible powerful
   woman.

Dear Parents,

I, like your daughter, was once a troubled teen - a very troubled teen. My parents, like you, were loving, intelligent people who tried everything they knew to make things better. Finally, at their wits' end, they sent me to an emotional growth/wilderness program much like New Horizons.

**That program changed my life.**

No, it wasn't a cure-all. But I turned a corner, and started on a healthier path and I am now living a happy successful life. My mission is to help bring that same kind of clarity and direction to your daughter, in the natural beauty of northern Maine.

You're thinking about entrusting your daughter to New Horizons for several weeks. That's a big decision, both emotionally and financially. I believe it may alleviate your concerns if you understand why I have such a passion for working with troubled young women. Here's my story:

I grew up in New York City. I was adopted at birth by two wonderful, hard working, highly influential parents. My parents told me from the day I came home that I was special, I was meant to be with them, I was "born in their hearts." I knew I was loved.

However, over the years, that high-powered environment took a toll on my sense of self. It wasn't my parents fault. I simply never felt like I really fit into the life that was chosen for me.

As a result of this "identity crisis," I began making very poor choices as a teenager - decisions that not only hurt me, but my family as well. I tested life in many ways that could have easily led to the end of my life. Thankfully, my parents enrolled me in a wilderness program much like New Horizons.

At first, being taken out of my environment only made me more confused and frustrated. But as the days went on, I was able to see my life more clearly. That program allowed me to step away from the "noise" of life, giving me time to breathe my own breath and realize it was okay to be me. The power of that seemingly simple realization changed my life.

New Horizons isn't a program for "fixing" your daughter. She is not broken. But she is most likely confused, angry and/or depressed-and in no shape to begin the hard work of getting her life back on track. Our job at New Horizons is to provide the rest, reflection and resolve she needs to start making better choices.

I encourage you to print and read over our website, send for our brochures, and call our office with any questions.

Then, if your better wisdom tells you to send your daughter to New Horizons, I encourage you to listen. My parents did. That's why we're here today for you.

Jacqueline Danforth
Founder, Executive Director

Dear Young Lady:

Your Mom or Dad have asked you to look at this website because they're worried about you.

Probably, in your moments of complete honesty, you're a little worried yourself.

You need to know some things. First, you're not alone. Many, many young women like you have struggles. I was one of them. I, like you, did and said some things that people weren't too happy with. But it was like I was riding a bike down a hill with no brakes. I didn't know how to stop myself from making destructive, negative choices.

**Luckily, my parents stepped in before I "crashed."**
I was brought to the woods, literally kicking and screaming. But in the end, that's where I experienced the first peace with myself I had had in years.

New Horizons can be that kind of place for you. Our goal is not to "reprogram" you or set you straight. It's a place where you can get down to the bare essentials. No phones, no make-up, no traffic lights and street noise.

Together with caring, safe adults and girls like yourself, you'll paddle a canoe, cook over a campfire, see more stars than you ever knew existed. When you're ready, we'll talk about your life, your frustrations, your dreams. Without all the people and activities and "junk noise" around you, you're going to get reacquainted with the most amazing person: **You.**

**I can't wait to meet you!**

*Jackie*

*No one can make you feel inferior without your consent.*
*~ Eleanor Roosevelt*

# AFFIRMATIONS

"Don't water your weeds." ~ Harvey MacKay

You are what you think. Whatever you believe with feeling becomes your reality. If you wish to change your reality, keep your conscious mind focused on positive thoughts. Affirming brings about the fastest and most dramatic changes in your life. You can change the mind's programming this way. Like seeds, the affirmations are planted in the mental garden and bear fruit in their own time. It will be work at first uprooting die-hard thoughts of doubts and negativities. But soon even the pluckiest ones surrender to consistently applied new thoughts and a beautiful garden of deep delight and insight will take root and grow.

Sometimes it is difficult because the mind's conditioning is rooted deep, and works without our knowing it, but anything that can be conditioned can be unconditioned. The moment you catch your self being negative, affirm that all is well ~ all is happening exactly as it should – and you can handle anything that comes your way. Make affirming the most important event of your day ~ around which all revolve.

Here are some examples. Change them to reflect whatever you want to attract into your life. Daily, repeat your chosen affirmations twenty times in succession with feeling. Don't do it by rote. Believe that the desired result is already achieved.

- I am an open, loving, creative person.
- I am free to create my reality.
- Everything I need is within me.
- I am radiantly healthy and vibrantly alive.
- I accept my feelings and am willing to express them.
- I communicate clearly and effectively.
- I enjoy loving relationships with my family and friends.
- All things are working together for my highest good.

Write your favorite affirmation on a separate page. Hang it in a place you pass throughout the day, so each time you see it you experience the thought anew. As you build your inner world with daily affirmations, wonderful changes in consciousness occur. Your commitment to mastering your mental forces instead of being controlled by them, benefits your life, your friends, your family, and your community. Try it for thirty days! The results will surprise you!

# Believe

Believe, pursue and carry through!
These are the things that you must do.
When the going is tough and you hesitate,
That's the very time you must not wait.
For in that moment what is done,
Determines if you've lost or won.
We can all be brave when the critics rave,
And friends crowd round to laud us,
But what about those times of doubt
With no one to applaud us?
Be your own best friend
For it's then you'll win,
So do what a friend would do:
Tell yourself you're great and appreciate
The things you say to you.
Do your part when heartaches start,
Don't worry about the rest.
Stay inspired although you're tired ~
Bring forth your very best.
If you're wondering what to do,
Don't even stop to ask.
Believe, pursue and carry through,
Your three-fold, life-long task!

© Pat Sampson

# CHARLES A. WEISS, DVM

**Dr. Charles A. Weiss** is a pioneer among veterinarians. Not only has he developed a very successful veterinary practice with an innovative, empathetic team approach to veterinary medicine, but he is also known for his powerful ability as an effective leader and insightful motivator.

Dr. Weiss' veterinary practice is unique in many ways. The high level of skill and the sincere empathy displayed by his entire staff has earned the practice the reputation as a friendly, patient-centered hospital. This, coupled with the latest technological advances and equipment, brings his patients state of the art medical care in a safe, nurturing environment. The pulse of the practice is the Bradley Hills Animal Hospital mission statement and a list of clinic values to which all staff members adhere: respect, honesty, integrity, teamwork, trust, courtesy, peacefulness and humility.

Dr. Weiss' deep level of understanding of the driving force of humans has enabled him to become a recognized leader and effective motivator. He shares his experiences and knowledge in many different venues including lectures, published articles and in his own practice. By doing so he helps others become centered, passionately motivated and deeply fulfilled. His philosophy includes living a balanced, happy life. To obtain this goal one must always focus on the positive in our lives, take full responsibility for our actions and adhere to our own values on a consistent basis. In addition, we must know we can obtain any goal if we are committed to the outcome, and believe in our own abilities.

Charles Weiss can be reached at
*www.Bradleyhills.com*
Bradley Hills Animal Hospital
Bethesda, Maryland
(301) 365-5448

# In Search of Fulfillment

*Although the outcome of our goals is important,*
*if we enjoy the process of everything we do,*
*we can truly enrich our lives.*

~ Dr. Charles Weiss

Are you living on a day-to-day basis, just getting by, or are you living a meaningful life in which each new day is an exciting adventure where you finish the day content and happy? Emotional fulfillment can be obtained by anyone with an open mind and a yearning to be completely satisfied. There are so many people who are financially and professionally successful but who feel empty inside and lack that warm feeling of fulfillment.

The following are questions and answers, which if read and eventually accepted, can lead any man or woman toward lifelong emotional fulfillment. Although your answers may at first be very different from these, allow yourself consciously - and eventually subconsciously - to accept these empowering ideas. Try reading each question and answer every night before going to sleep. Over time, your mind will more readily accept their truth.

### How do I want to feel?

You must realize that you deserve to feel great every day. It can't be a wish or a "should be;" it has to be a *must*. If your answer is *"I am committed to doing what is necessary to feel happiness, respect, love and satisfaction every day,"* then continue.

### Who is responsible for my sense of feeling fulfilled?

You have to truly understand and believe that you are not a victim of circumstance. You are totally in control of how you feel on a daily basis. If you want to feel happy and satisfied, hold no other person except yourself responsible for how you feel. Don't be one of those people who go through life with a "poor me" attitude focusing on how bad you have it or how others hurt you. It is your responsibility to focus on the positive in your life, independent of what others might say. Don't let yourself think "he/she made me mad." You must decide to take control of how you feel. If your answer is *"I will now be responsible for how I feel and work every day to ensure that I am totally fulfilled"*, then continue.

### Can I control my focus (or what I think about every day)?

Definitely. If you frequently find yourself unhappy, sad, fearful or worried, your focus is on things over which you have no control or the potentially negative things that could happen. Your thoughts (focus) are made up of the questions you ask yourself minute to minute. If you ask yourself: "Why am I fat?" you are affirming you are fat. The only reason you would ask yourself a question like this is if you want to make yourself feel bad. But none of us should want to feel bad.

You must learn to ask yourself empowering questions everyday. If you look for and focus on the good, you will feel good. If you focus on the negative you will feel sad and depressed and not have the motivation to do all the great things of which you are capable. One way to set up a new pattern of positive thinking is to ask yourself every morning: "what's good about my life?" and "what am I excited about today?"

### How do I tend to my basic needs?

There are several basic needs that you must satisfy if you want to find fulfillment. Certainty about what makes you feel safe and comfortable is one of the most important. Although there is not enough space to discuss each in great detail, the following are some definite steps to take. Your response to these basic needs must come only from yourself. You must not be influenced by the opinion of other people unless you want others to control your focus and your fulfillment.

For example, do not give any weight to another's opinion regarding the question "Am I important?" As long as the negative opinions of others are important to you, you will never find fulfillment. You must set up the rules of the game. Rather then compare yourself to anyone else ~ focus your energy on feeling good about who you are ~ and who you will become.

## CERTAINTY

Certainty is feeling assured about your future, safety, comfort and significance. If you are uncertain about any of these things, you will feel anxious, fearful or worried, which will lead to a feeling of overwhelm, depression or anger.

To be fulfilled is to be certain about several areas of your life. *These include your appearance, your importance/self worth, your personal growth/development, your purpose and your contribution to the greater good.* If you are certain about how you feel in these areas, your answers will empower you and lead to greater satisfaction. If your answers are not positive, ask "how can I make it better?" and immediately take steps to achieve this goal. If you instead have negative answers to these questions and do nothing to change your perceptions, you are making a conscious decision to stay negative. Allow yourself to answer these questions in a positive way if you want to feel good about yourself.

### *Certainty of Appearance*

Our physical appearance is the first thing people see when we meet them. Although it is far more important who we are inside, it is important that we decide to be comfortable about our appearance no matter what it may be. Remember, it is your opinion that is most important; it doesn't matter what anyone else thinks. When you begin to place yourself in the hands of a beautiful principle in which you appreciate who you are ~ faith in yourself strengthens ~ and you have the power to overcome the opinions of others and your perceptions about their opinions.

### *What about my appearance do I like best?*

_____

_____

_____

_____

_____

**If you are not happy with your appearance, ask yourself ~ *What could I like about my appearance if I wanted to?***

_____

_____

_____

*How do I want to look and why?*

_____

_____

_____

*What are three positive changes I can make as part of my daily routine, which would allow me to move toward my goal while enjoying the process.*

**(Examples – establishing a different eating routine or adding some form of exercise into your day.)**

_____

_____

_____

### Certainty of Importance/Self Worth

Even with the best-intentioned parents, many of us did not have our emotional needs completely met as children. As a result, we might lack a strong sense of self worth, and pride in who we are. It is of paramount importance to love and respect ourselves before we can feel loved, respected and important. Our thoughts are the primary causes of the conditions of our lives, and if we wish our lives to be different in the future, we have to change our thinking in the present.

*What are some of the positive qualities I have that make me feel good about myself?*

_____

_____

_____

_____

*Why do I feel important?*

_____

_____

_____

_____

*What values do I live by that I am most proud of in my life (examples – respect, honesty, integrity)*

_____

_____

_____

_____

_____

### *Certainty of Personal Growth/Development*

To feel fulfilled, you must continue to grow emotionally, physically, and spiritually. The time you grow most is after facing and overcoming a problem or challenge. You must never allow yourself to think and say to others "why did this happen to me?" Instead if you focus on the solution you will have the opportunity to grow to a new level of understanding, knowledge and ability to grow stronger; able to do more than you ever realized. When you face a challenge, ask: *"what can I learn from this?"*

*In what areas can I continue to grow?*

_____

_____

_____

_____

*What are three steps I could take today which will enable me to grow (emotionally, physically and spiritually) and enjoy the process?*

_____

_____

_____

_____

*What are specific ways I can grow in these areas (books, tapes, school, modeling the behavior of others who are successful)?*

_____

_____

_____

_____

## PURPOSE

The need for meaning and purpose is the greatest single drive in human nature. To have the life we want to have we must first know where we are going. Without a purpose, we are like a rowboat without oars. With a purpose we know what we want to achieve and can help shape our destiny. To feel fulfilled it is important that we not only achieve our desired outcome, but also enjoy the process of everything we do. Once we understand the process, we have to make an effort to apply what we have learned to achieve far higher levels of fulfillment in our daily lives.

*What do I feel is my primary purpose in life?*

_____

_____

_____

*What are the things I enjoy most doing?*

_____

_____

_____

*What would I like to be doing in five, ten, and twenty years?*

_____

_____

_____

*What changes can I make to achieve these outcomes?*

_____

_____

_____

## CONTRIBUTION TO THE GREATER GOOD

Finally to be totally satisfied in life, we must have a sense that we are making a genuine contribution to society. This is possible for each of us, whether we contribute by being a giving, supportive person, or by inventing something of value to humankind. We must have a sense that our lives are about more than just what we can get. If we live our lives taking, but never giving in return, we cannot feel fulfilled.

*How can I contribute to the greater good?*

_____

_____

_____

*How can I be a positive role model for others?*

_____

_____

_____

*Name five ways that my life can make a difference (start at home – smiling every day, transfer positive energy to others, respect other people I come in contact with, be more supportive of others).*

_____

_____

_____

_____

_____

### *What to do when stressed or overwhelmed*

All control over our circumstances begins with taking control of the thoughts we hold in our conscious minds. Anytime you feel stressed about a situation or event, you can take yourself out of that feeling of loss of control and overwhelm by focusing on and answering the following questions:

### *What am I certain about in this situation?*

_____

_____

_____

### *What can I do to make it as good as possible?*

_____

_____

_____

### *What can I learn from this?*

_____

_____

_____

It is imperative that we spend 95% of our time thinking about the solution. If we continue to think about, and focus on a problem and all the potential negative things which could happen we will feel anxious, fearful and out of control. If we focus on how to fix the problem and what things we can do next time to avoid the problem, we will feel more complete. If we ask ourselves empowering questions every day, our minds will create a new pattern that will help lead us to a feeling of personal fulfillment.

# THE TREASURE OF TIME

*"You can always get another car, or another diamond.*
*But you can't get back the minute you just lost."*

~ Ray Charles

If you awoke one morning and found on your doorstep a treasure chest brimming with sparkling diamonds, rubies, and pearls, what would you do? Would you scatter the contents up and down the sidewalk to be trampled underfoot? Would you give it away indiscriminately? Or would you appreciate your newly acquired fortune and carefully determine how to put it to its best use?

Each morning you are presented a fortune greater than diamonds ~ a treasure sparkling, new, and irreplaceable. Do you greet your gift with a dull yawn of boredom, hardly noticing the richness that awaits? Do you accept it complacently, taking it for granted? Or do you make every effort to get the most from your day?

Time is your most valuable possession. You need time to dream, to plan, to work. Time to set goals and reach them; time to learn, to grow, to face challenges, to overcome obstacles. As you go about your day, focus your attention on the present moment. The past may hold lessons and the future promise, but only the present offers the opportunity to act. Invest your riches wisely, trading your wealth of seconds, minutes, and hours only for something of value. You would not trade your most valuable diamond for a synthetic stone, no matter how brightly it shone, because you would be exchanging items of unequal value. So it is with the activities for which you barter your time.

You would not cancel an important business meeting to go shopping; that is an obvious imbalance of priorities. And how about spending time wishing you had more money when you could be earning it ~ or using a large block of time for five small disjointed projects instead of that one big project you've been meaning to get under way? Save rainy day projects for rainy days and make use of the sunlight while it is yours.

# LIFE

*"There are only two ways to live your life.*
*One is as though nothing is a miracle.*
*The other is as though everything is a miracle."*
~ Albert Einstein

Life ~ let me love you. You are everything to me. Let me not take you for granted for there is no substitute for you. You are a ripple in the stream of eternity that cannot be explained or understood. I seek not to explain you, only to love you, for your existence is my existence. As long as you continue to be, I continue to be.

Of all loves, you are the most constant, the most faithful, the most enduring and yet the most fickle. You give the illusion of forever but forever you cannot stay. I value your priceless seconds, golden days and hours, more than bank accounts, oil wells or diamond mines. I welcome every opportunity to gain knowledge, insight, and understanding. I seek relationships with others eager to learn and grow. I thank you for the gift of reason and understanding.

For no matter whose influence touches my life, my own experiences remain my greatest teacher. I accept responsibility for myself and make empowering choices that govern the course of my life. I have a strong sense of well-being and become the best that I can be. If I really believe that I create my own reality, I will.

I have such an abundance of miracles in my life. I live each moment discovering anew the beauty of the world around me. I love and respect all of life. I get that we are all part of the same sacred energy ~ human beings, animals, and Mother Earth herself. I cherish the people I love and who love me. I know that no matter what my experiences or desires may be ~ family and friends are the most important gifts of all.

As the last seconds of the day disappear, thoughts of abundance, love and joy sink deep into my consciousness, so that tomorrow I awaken with passion and purpose because we are together again.

# LOUISE L. HAY

**Louise L. Hay** is a metaphysical lecturer and teacher and the bestselling author of 27 books, including *You Can Heal Your Life* and *Empowering Women*. Her works have been translated into 25 different languages in 33 countries throughout the world. Since beginning her career as a Science of Mind minister in 1981, Louise has assisted thousands of people in discovering and using the full potential of their own creative powers for personal growth and self-healing.

Louise is the founder and chairman of Hay House, Inc., a publishing company that began in the living room of her home which now disseminates millions of books, audios, and videos that contribute to the healing of the planet. The Hay Foundation and the Louise L. Hay Charitable Fund are two nonprofit organizations established by Louise, which support many diverse organizations including those dealing with aids, battered women and other disadvantaged individuals in our society.

She has appeared on television around the world, and her monthly column, *"Dear Louise,"* appears in over 50 publications in the United States, Canada, Australia, Spain and Argentina. Through her healing techniques and positive philosophy, millions have learned how to create more of what they want in their lives, including more wellness in their bodies, minds and spirit.

*You Can Heal Your Life* **by Louise L. Hay.**
**Published by Hay House, Inc.,**
**is available at all bookstores.**
**Phone 800-654-5126, or go to** *www.hayhouse.com*

# What I Believe

*Life is very simple. What we give out, we get back.* I believe that everyone, myself included, is responsible for every experience in our lives, the best and the worst. Every thought we think is creating our future. Each one of us creates our experiences by the thoughts we think and the words we speak and the beliefs we hold.

Beliefs are ideas and thoughts that we accept as truth. What we think about ourselves and the world becomes true for us. What we choose to believe can expand and enrich our world. Each day can be an exciting, joyous, hopeful experience; or a sorrowful, limiting, and painful one. Two people living in the same world, with the same set of circumstances, can experience life so differently. What can transport us from one world to another? I'm convinced that it's our beliefs that do so. When we're willing to change our primary belief structures, then we may experience a true change in our lives.

Whatever your beliefs may be about yourself and the world, remember that they're only thoughts, and thoughts can be changed. You may not agree with some of the ideas that I'm about to explore. Some of them may be unfamiliar and frightening. Don't worry. Only those ideas that are right for you will become part of you. You may think that some of the techniques are too simple or foolish and could not possibly work for you. I'm only asking you to try them.

*Our subconscious mind accepts whatever we choose to believe.* The Universal Power never judges or criticizes us. It only accepts us at our own value. If you accept a limiting belief, then it will become the truth for you. If you believe that you're too short, too fat, too thin, too tall, too smart, not smart enough, too rich, too poor, or incapable of forming relationships, then those beliefs will become true for you.

Remember that we're dealing with thoughts, and thoughts can be changed. We have unlimited choices about what we can think, and the point of power is always in the present moment.

What are you thinking in the present moment? Is it positive or negative? Do you want this thought to be creating your future?

51

*When we were children, we learned about life and about ourselves from the reactions of the adults around us.* Therefore, most of us have ideas about who we are that were merely someone else's opinions. And we have many rules about how life "should" be lived. If you lived with people who were unhappy, frightened, guilty, or angry, then you learned a lot of negative things about yourself and your world.

*When we grow up, we have a tendency to re-create the emotional environment of our early home life.* We also tend to re-create in our personal relationships the ones we had with our mother and father. If we were highly criticized or abused as children, then we will seek out those individuals in our adult life who will duplicate this behavior. If we were praised, loved, and encouraged as children, then we will re-create those patterns.

*I do not encourage you to blame your parents.* We are all victims of victims, and they couldn't teach you something that they didn't know. If your mother or father didn't know how to love themselves, it would have been impossible for them to teach *you* how to love yourself. They were coping as best they could with the information they had. Think for a minute about how they were raised. If you want to understand your parents more, I suggest that you ask them about their childhoods.

Listen to not only *what* they're telling you, but notice what happens to them *while* they're speaking. What is their body language like? Can they make eye contact with you? Look into their eyes and see if you can find their inner child. You may only see it for a split second, but it may reveal some valuable information.

*I believe that we choose our parents.* I believe that we've decided to incarnate on this earth in a particular time and space. We've come here to learn specific lessons that will advance us on our spiritual, evolutionary pathway. I believe that we choose our sex, color, and country, and then we search for the particular set of parents who will enhance our spiritual work in this lifetime.

*All that we're dealing with is a thought, and a thought can be changed.* No matter what the problem is, your experiences are outer effects of inner thoughts. Even self-hatred is only a thought you have about yourself. This thought produces a feeling, and you buy into that feeling. However, if you don't have the thought, you won't have the feeling. Thoughts can be changed. Change the thought, and the feeling most go.

The past has no power over us. It doesn't matter how long we've been in a negative pattern. We can be free in this moment.

*Believe it or not, we do choose our thoughts.* We may habitually think the same thought over and over so that it doesn't seem as if we're choosing the thought. But we did make the original choice. We can refuse to think certain thoughts. How often have you refused to think a positive thought about yourself? You can also refuse to think a negative thought about yourself.

*The innermost belief for everyone that I've worked with is always, "I'm not good enough!"* Everyone that I know or have worked with is suffering from self-hatred or guilt to one degree or another. "I'm not good enough, I don't do enough, or I don't deserve this," are common complaints. But for whom are you not good enough? And by whose standards?

*I find that resentment, criticism, guilt, and fear cause most of the problems in ourselves and in our lives.* These feelings come from blaming others and not taking responsibility for our own experiences. If we're all responsible for everything in our lives, then there's no one to blame. Whatever is happening "out there" is only a mirror of our own inner thinking.

I do not condone other people's poor behavior, but it's our own belief system that attracts this behavior to us. There's some thought in you that attracts people who exhibit abusive behavior. If you find that people are constantly mistreating you, then this is your belief pattern. When you change the thought that attracts this behavior, it will stop.

*We can change our attitudes toward the past.* It's over and done and can't be changed. Yet we *can* change our thoughts about the past. How foolish for us to punish ourselves in the present moment because someone hurt us long ago. If we choose to believe that we're helpless victims and that it's all hopeless, then the Universe will support us in that belief. Our worst opinions of ourselves will be confirmed.

If we choose to believe that we're responsible for our experiences, the good and the so-called bad, then we have the opportunity to outgrow the effects of the past. We can change. We can be free.

*The road to freedom is through the doorway to forgiveness.* We may not know how to forgive, and we may not *want* to forgive; but if we're *willing* to forgive, we may begin the healing process. It's imperative for our own healing that we release the past and forgive everyone.

I'm not saying that it's all right that someone behaved in a misguided way. However, we must be aware that the past is over. We only carry the hurt and the memory in our mind. This is what we want to let go of – the pain we're continuing to cause ourselves because we won't forgive. Forgiveness means giving up, letting go. We understand our own pain so well, yet it's hard for most of us to understand the pain of someone who treated us badly. That person we need to forgive was also in pain. And they're only mirroring what *we* believed about ourselves. They were doing the best they could, given the knowledge, understanding, and awareness they possessed at the time.

When people come to me with a problem – I don't care what it is – poor health, lack of money, unfulfilling relationships, or stifled creativity – there's only one thing that I ever work on, and that is *loving the self.*

I find that when we really love, accept, and approve of ourselves exactly as we are, everything in life flows. Joyous self-approval and self-acceptance in the here and now are the keys to positive change in every area of our lives.

*To me, loving the self means never, ever criticizing ourselves for anything.* Criticism locks us into the very pattern we're trying to change.

Try approving of yourself and see what happens. You've been criticizing yourself for years. Has it worked?

# Exercises:

## *LISTEN TO YOURSELF*

This exercise requires a tape recorder. Tape your telephone conversations for a week or so – just your voice. When the tape is filled on both sides, sit down and listen to it. Listen to not only what you say, but the way you say it. What are your beliefs? Who and what do you criticize? Which parent, if any, do you sound like?

As you release the need to pick on yourself all the time, you'll notice that you no longer criticize others so much.

When you make it okay to be yourself, then you automatically allow others to be themselves. Their little habits no longer bother you so much. You release the need to change them. As you stop judging *others*, they release the need to judge you. Everybody wants to be free.

You may be a person who criticizes everyone around you. And if you do, you will certainly criticize yourself, too. So you may ask yourself:

1. What do I get from being angry all the time?

_____

_____

_____

_____

2. What happens if I let go of my anger?

_____

_____

_____

_____

3. Am I willing to forgive and be free?

_____

_____

_____

_____

## *WRITE A LETTER*

Think of someone whom you're still angry with. Perhaps it's an old anger. Write this person a letter. Tell them all your grievances and how you feel. Don't hold back. Really express yourself.

When you've finished the letter, read it once, then fold it, and on the outside write: "What I really want is your love and approval." Then burn the letter and release it.

## *MIRROR WORK*

Think of another person, or even the same person once again, whom you're angry with. Sit down in front of a mirror. Be sure to have some tissues nearby. Look into your own eyes and "see" the other person. Tell them what you're so angry about.

When you're finished, tell them, "What I really want is your love and approval." We're all seeking love and approval. That's what we want from everyone, and that's what everyone wants from us. Love and approval bring harmony into our lives.

In order to be free, we need to release the old ties that bind us. So once again look into the mirror and affirm to yourself, "I am willing to release the need to be an angry person." Notice if you're really willing to let go, or if you're holding onto the past.

The statements listed below are examples of self-defeating beliefs, along with the positive affirmation corresponding to each belief. Make these affirmations part of your daily routine. Say them often in the car, at work, while looking in the mirror, or any time that you feel your negative beliefs surfacing.

| If You Believe: | Your Affirmation Could Be: |
|---|---|
| People are so stupid. | *Everybody is doing the best they can, including me.* |
| I'd do it if I weren't so fat. | *I appreciate the wonder of my body.* |
| Those are the ugliest clothes I've ever seen. | *I love the uniqueness that people express in their clothing.* |
| They'll never be able to finish the job. | *I release the need to criticize others.* |
| I'm such a klutz. | *I become more proficient every day.* |
| If I get angry, I'll lose control. | *I express my anger in appropriate places and ways.* |
| I have no right to be angry. | *All my emotions are acceptable.* |
| Anger is bad. | *Anger is normal and natural.* |
| When someone is angry, I get scared. | *I comfort my inner child, and we are safe.* |
| It's not safe to be angry. | *I am safe with all my emotions.* |
| I won't be loved if I get mad. | *The more honest I am, the more I am loved.* |
| Stuffing anger makes me sick. | *I allow myself freedom with all my emotions, including anger.* |
| I've never been angry. | *Healthy expressions of anger keep me healthy.* |
| My neighbors are so noisy. | *I release the need to be disturbed.* |
| Nobody asks me what I think. | *My opinions are valued.* |

"I give myself permission to acknowledge my feelings."

Good mental health begins with loving the self. When we love and approve of ourselves completely ~ the good and the so-called bad ~ we can begin to change.

# MARTIN E.P. SELIGMAN, PH.D

**Martin E.P. Seligman, Ph.D.**, is Fox Leadership Professor of Psychology in the Department of Psychology at the University of Pennsylvania. He is well known in academic and clinical circles and is the best-selling author of twenty books translated into sixteen languages. Among his better-known works are *Authentic Happiness; Learned Optimism; What You Can Change & What You Can't; The Optimistic Child; Helplessness;* and *Abnormal Psychology* with David Rosenhan.

In 1996 Dr. Seligman was elected President of the American Psychological Association, by the largest vote in modern history. His primary aim as APA President was to join practice and science together so both might flourish, a goal that has dominated his own life as a psychologist. His major initiatives concerned the prevention of ethnopolitical warfare and the study of Positive Psychology.

Since 2000 his main mission has been the promotion of the field of Positive Psychology. This discipline includes the study of positive emotion, positive character traits, and positive institutions. As the science behind these becomes more firmly grounded, Dr. Seligman is now turning his attention to training Positive Psychologists, individuals whose practice will make the world a happier place.

*www.authentichappinesscoaching.com,*
*www.authentichappiness.org*

# POSITIVE PSYCHOLOGY

Positive Psychology is not a luxury whose benefits will accrue only to the rich, to the secure, and to the untroubled. Positive Psychology seeks to understand and build three kinds of happy lives: the Pleasant Life, the Good Life, and the Meaningful Life. Some, but not many, aspects of these lives are perhaps more easily partaken by those not in pain: the taste of caviar or a day of skiing, for example.

But most of Positive Psychology is for all of us, troubled or untroubled, privileged or in privation, suffering or carefree. The pleasures of a good conversation, the strength of gratitude, the benefits of kindness or wisdom or spirituality or humility, the search for meaning and the antidote to "fidgeting until we die" are the birthrights of us all.

**Another arrow in the quiver**

Positive Psychology is not remotely intended as a replacement for psychology-as-usual. Clinical psychology and biological psychiatry have amply demonstrated that they can make the lives of suffering people less unhappy. Fourteen of the major mental illnesses are relievable today and two are curable; none were treatable fifty years ago. This work must and surely will go on. The severely depressed, single mother is one of its many beneficiaries. But she is also concerned with integrity, meaning, kindness, and being a good parent and citizen.

We overcome our suffering not only by healing damage and repairing what is broken within ourselves. More commonly we overcome troubles by doing end-runs around them, by deploying our highest strengths as buffers against the setbacks of life. And these domains-buffering, strength, pleasure, and meaning – long neglected by psychology-as-usual, are the subject matter of Positive Psychology.

So Positive Psychology seeks not to replace, but to add another arrow into the quiver of clinical psychology, biological psychiatry, psychiatric social work, marriage and family counseling, and coaching. In the last five years, Positive Psychology has discovered interventions that build more happiness by nurturing the Pleasant Life, the Good Life, and the Meaningful Life.

Research on positive psychology provides compelling evidence that individuals can increase their happiness by identifying and engaging in their signature strengths. The more we use these strengths, the more steadily we advance into the Good Life, a life of immersion, absorption, and flow.

## VALUES IN ACTION SIGNATURE STRENGTHS.

These are the 24 strengths in the VIA Signature Strengths Survey talked about in my book *Authentic Happiness*. The strengths are grouped by the virtues that they support.

## WISDOM AND KNOWLEDGE
*Cognitive strengths that entail the acquisition and use of knowledge*

- **Creativity**
  Thinking of novel and productive ways to do things; includes artistic achievement but is not limited to it

- **Curiosity**
  Taking an interest in all of ongoing experience; finding all subjects and topics fascinating; exploring and discovering

- **Open-mindedness**
  Thinking things through and examining them from all sides; not jumping to conclusions; being able to change one's mind in light of evidence; weighing all evidence fairly

- **Love of Learning**
  Mastering new skills, topics, and bodies of knowledge, whether on one's own or formally. Obviously related to the strength of curiosity but goes beyond it to describe the tendency to add systematically to what one knows

- **Perspective**
  Being able to provide wise counsel to others; having ways of looking at the world that make sense to the self and to other people

## COURAGE
*Emotional strengths that involve the exercise of will to accomplish goals in the face of opposition, external or internal*

- **Bravery**
  Not shrinking from threat, challenge, difficulty, or pain; speaking up for what is right even if there is opposition; acting on convictions even if unpopular; includes physical bravery but is not limited to it

- **Industry/Perseverance**
  Finishing what one starts; persisting in a course of action in spite of obstacles; "getting it out the door"; taking pleasure in completing tasks

- **Authenticity**
  Speaking the truth but more broadly presenting oneself in a genuine way; being without pretense; taking responsibility for one's feelings and actions

- **Zest**
  Approaching life with excitement and energy; not doing things halfway or halfheartedly; living life as an adventure; feeling alive and activated

## LOVE
*Interpersonal strengths that involve "tending" and "befriending" others (Taylor et al., 2000)*

- **Intimacy**
  Valuing close relations with others, in particular those in which sharing and caring are reciprocated; being close to people

- **Kindness**
  Doing favors and good deeds for others; helping them; taking care of them

- **Social Intelligence**
  Being aware of the motives and feelings of other people and the self; knowing what to do to fit in to different social situations; knowing what makes other people tick

## JUSTICE
*Civic strengths that underlie healthy community life*

- **Citizenship/Teamwork**
  Working well as member of a group or team; being loyal to the group; doing one's share

- **Fairness**
  Treating all people the same according to notions of fairness and justice; not letting personal feelings bias decisions about others; giving everyone a fair chance

- **Leadership**
  Encouraging a group of which one is a member to get things done and at the same time good relations within the group; organizing group activities and seeing that they happen

## TEMPERANCE
*Strengths that protect against excess*

- **Forgiveness/Mercy**
  Forgiving those who have done wrong; giving people a second chance; not being vengeful

- **Modesty/Humility**
  Letting one's accomplishments speak for themselves; not seeking the spotlight; not regarding one's self as more special than one is

- **Prudence**
  Being careful about one's choices; not taking undue risks; not saying or doing things that might later be regretted

- **Self-control/Self-regulation**
  Regulating what one feels and does; being disciplined; controlling one's appetites and emotions

## TRANSCENDENCE
*Strengths that forge connections to the larger universe and provide meaning*

- **Awe/Appreciation of Beauty and Excellence**
Noticing and appreciating beauty, excellence, and/or skilled performance in all domains of life, from nature to art to mathematics to science to everyday experience

- **Gratitude**
Being aware of and thankful for the good things that happen; taking time to express thanks

- **Hope**
Expecting the best in the future and working to achieve it; believing that a good future is something that can be brought about

- **Playfulness**
Liking to laugh and tease; bringing smiles to other people; seeing the light side; making (not necessarily telling) jokes

- **Spirituality**
Having coherent beliefs about the higher purpose and meaning of the universe; knowing where one fits within the larger scheme; having beliefs about the meaning of life that shape conduct and provide comfort

## Using Our Signature Strengths

One of my signature strengths is a love of learning, and I am fortunate to be in a profession that allows me to use this strength on a daily – even hourly – basis. I've found that much of my learning goes on in the classroom – my classroom – as I interact with bright University of Pennsylvania undergraduate and graduate students. Since entering the field in 1964 I have had ample opportunities to indulge my love of learning by teaching in settings ranging from large university lecture halls to intimate seminar courses with only a handful of students. But this semester I tried something different....

# POSITIVE PSYCHOLOGY
# GOES TO COLLEGE

I teamed up with two of my colleagues – Dr. John Dilulio and Dr. Christopher Peterson – to teach an introductory course on positive psychology. As far as we know, this is the first time that a 100-level course in positive psychology has been taught on a university campus. The purpose of the course is to introduce students to the science behind positive psychology. We divide the material into positive emotions, positive character strengths, and positive institutions. The interdisciplinary content of the course attracted a diverse group of students interested in psychology, political science, communication, business, and other fields. Four hundred students competed for the 120 available places.

**Positive Emotions, Character Strengths, and Institutions**

During the first third of the course in the weekly two-hour lectures, I presented what is known about positive emotions. Christopher Peterson lectured during the second third of the course about positive character strengths. (Dr. Peterson is uniquely qualified to lead this endeavor because he is the first author of the *Values in Action Classification of Strengths,* a large-scale classification of strengths valued across cultures, UnDSM-1.) The final third of the course, which focused on positive institutions, is taught not by a psychology professor but rather by political science guru John Dilulio (former Director of the White House Office of Faith-Based and Community Initiatives and with Judy Rodin my fellow Robert Fox Professor of Leadership at Penn).

**Not The Typical Course**

The weekly section meetings allowed me the privilege of witnessing firsthand the students' excitement as they realized they were not in a "typical" university course with an exclusive emphasis on book learning. Half of their homework consisted of exercises in which they apply the science to their own lives. For example, in one section of the course students practiced specific savoring techniques (designed to enhance positive emotion in the present) by lingering over a meal, relishing a recent success (rather than immediately moving on to their next task), and losing themselves in the melody of a favorite song.

During the part of the course devoted to the study of character strengths, students learn to identify their signature strengths and use these strengths to transform boring tasks and to enhance their leisure time. Toward the end of the course, homework exercises challenge students to articulate the people, activities, and beliefs that give them a stronger sense of meaning and purpose for their lives. Each student does exercises that involve giving the gift of time, forgiving a wrong, expressing gratitude to others, mentoring another student, and serving their community. These practical exercises require written observations and evaluations in order to encourage the students to give thoughtful, sustained attention to their positive experiences and of course there are no right or wrong answers.

Not the typical undergraduate survey course!

**I Know Things Will Be Different Now**

So what was the impact on the students? Did students leave this course not only more knowledgeable about the subject but actually *happier* as well? The official results will be in soon. At the beginning of the course, students completed a series of questionnaires about their baseline levels of happiness and life satisfaction. Students will retake these same questionnaires at the end of the course and again one year later. But in the meantime, I am content to savor the mountain of anecdotal evidence provided by my students of the positive (and sometimes profound) impact this course has had on their lives. Let me close with an example of one exercise and the effect it had on my students. The assignment given to the students was as follows....

*Imagine that one day, long after you have passed away, one of your great grandchildren asks about you and your life. How would you want to be remembered and described? Write a summary of your life (one page) as you would like to have it related to your great grandchild. Be sure to include a description of your values and your personal characteristics. Put this summary aside for a few days and then come back to it. Notice not only what you included in your summary but also what you omitted. Are there activities that consume a great deal of time in your waking life that you did not include in the summary? Why did you leave them out? What changes might you make in your life so that this life summary might one day be an accurate reflection of your life and personal priorities?*

Almost all of my students reported that they found this experience helpful in that it helped them to "get my priorities straight" or that it "made me realize that I was spending too much time worrying about what doesn't matter and not enough time worrying about what does." The journal entry of one student in particular stands out in my mind, and I would like to close by sharing with you her reaction to the exercise:

*"I simply was not prepared for my emotional reaction to this exercise. I sat down with my pen and paper and began to cry. At first I cried over the realization that for the past several years I have been utterly neglecting what used to be such an important part of my life. And then I cried out of relief because I know things will be different now...."*

© Martin E. P. Seligman, Ph.D. all rights reserved

# Great Thoughts

### Robert Louis Stevenson
If a man is honest with others and with himself
If he receives gratefully and gives quietly
If he is gentle enough to feel
and strong enough to show his feelings
If he is slow to see the faults of others
but quick to discover their goodness
If he is cheerful in difficult times and modest in success
If he does his best to be true to his beliefs
Then he is truly an admirable man.

### Marianne Williamson
If something makes your heart sing, that's God's way of telling you
it's a contribution He wants you to make. Sharing our gifts is what
makes us happy. We're most powerful, and God's power is most
apparent on the earth, when we're happy.

### Martin Luther King, Jr.
If a man is called to be a street sweeper, he should sweep streets
even as Michelangelo painted, or Beethoven composed music, or
Shakespeare wrote poetry. He should sweep streets so well that
all the hosts of heaven and earth will pause to say, here lived
a great street sweeper who did his job well.

### Albert Einstein
The important thing is not to stop questioning. Curiosity has its
own reason for existing. One cannot help but be in awe when he
contemplates the mysteries of eternity, of life, of the marvelous
structure of reality. It is enough if one tries merely to comprehend
a little of this mystery everyday. Never lose a holy curiosity.

### Sir Winston Churchill
One ought never to turn one's back on a threatened danger and
try to run away from it. If you do that, you will double the danger.
But if you meet it promptly and without flinching, you will reduce
the danger by half. Never run away from anything. Never!

### Barbara J. Burrow
That woman is a success who loves life and lives it to the fullest; who
has discovered and shared the strengths and talents that are uniquely
her own; who puts her best into each task and leaves each situation
better than she found it; who seeks and finds that which is beautiful in
all people and all things; whose heart is full of love and warm with
compassion; who has found joy in living and peace within herself.

### Helen Keller
No pessimist ever discovered the secret of the stars,
or sailed to an uncharted land,
or opened a new doorway for the human spirit.

# Dorothy W. Morgan-Quelch

This author of the stage script "Looking for a Church in America"® epitomizes a curious mix of poise and pizzazz! In conversation she shares a strong sense of purpose that is imbued in her self-styled enterprise — MS PROTOCOL INC.™ She explained "MS" is an acronym for the multiple services that she provides and "PROTOCOL" as the name itself suggests, exacts order, due respect, and discipline. After 35 years of service to international organizations Dorothy is the recipient of various community service awards and letters of appreciation.

"Life has dealt me a good hand," she insists "there is much more to be gained." Her belief lies in the universal providence, as she is convinced of her role as a vessel for service to civilization. Traditions that today fuel the humanity in her venture are a fascinating childhood, with a father who had a passion for community service and a mother whose determination was to ensure that every generation in her family advanced ahead of the previous one.

She quotes, "I have traveled to Europe and every part of the Caribbean; lived in the United Kingdom for a number of years, and visited much of South and Central America, all in the pursuit of cultural awareness and diverse ethical principles. My quest now is to experience the rich multi-colored protocol of the African continent."

**For more information visit**
**MS PROTOCOL INC.**
at *www.protocol-events.com.*
Email *msprotocol@aol.com.*

**W**hen we hear the term protocol we immediately think of formality, this is a comprehensible misconception. What really should come to mind is how to? When to? And why should we? For protocol is the integration of creation, existence, and survival.

The most viable protocols of the universe are the seasons. As spring, summer, autumn, and winter cleanse and feed, living creatures experience psychological and physiological transformations. The seasons dictate the time to plant and to harvest; they influence every quadrant of life. Following creation, the protocol of life has remained the same; every living thing originates from an egg; from the egg comes the embryo that develops into the life form which blossoms, blooms, reproduces, and subsequently withers.

Children are trained to address their parents as Mom and Dad; these titles carry a sense of respect. Nevertheless, before a child could walk, talk or understand love, innocent children are aware of their dependence on parents and the innate protocol of survival begins its refinement gradually maturing with the evolving phases of life.

Let us turn to the protocol of language; it is quite clear that a good command of one's own language coupled with a varied vocabulary is a more powerful tool than any measure of crass behavior. A tactful facilitator structures his/her presentation on five basic principles, i.e., salutation, recognition, compliment, appreciation, and gratitude. Having a clear understanding of this formula is the gateway to social, political, and economic success.

On the social showground, weddings are a great example. Weddings take different platforms based on culture and location. Nevertheless, the protocol remains unchanged; two people deciding to share the rest of their lives together, the person who performs the ceremony, registration of the union, and a gathering of family and friends to celebrate the occasion.

Today's society is faced with discovering the protocol for harmonious coexistence among diverse cultures. Knowing that such protocols already exist is the advantage, our duty now is to identify and adapt those norms for the benefit of human dignity.

## Social

Our virtues speak for us on the showground of social protocol. Using the principles that were instilled in us from parents, grandparents, teachers, clergy, and our peers, we have become what we are. Putting it all together we select the qualities that best support our intrinsic worth.

Social protocol is a discipline of sorts, depending on where we set our goals. Our basic tools are knowledge, attitude, behavior, implementation, and effectiveness because the objective is to improve personal relationships and to treat others the way we wish to be treated.

To discuss this we rely on illustrations. First look at acquaintances and relationships. A good relationship thrives on compliment and support, when there is need for objection or rejection, it must be done with self-respect and tact. "You are not my type." should have no place in our social communication "I like you but I don't feel a chemistry," or "That is not where I am focused at the present time," articulates a much more refined individual.

When attending a job interview, the resume is always hand held; the only exception is a man's inside top jacket pocket. Dress appropriately for the position you are seeking, be punctual, and greet the potential employer with a firm single handshake.

In this era of comfortable T-shirts and jeans, sneakers and baseball caps, we continue to be judged by our appearance, the way we speak, and our attitude. It therefore behooves us to understand how to address the people we meet, why we walk ahead of our partner into a restaurant and choose the seat yet we ensure that the gentleman, or the host, gets the seat that faces the door, when to pick up the tab, how to identify ourselves when we telephone the opposite sex, and other principles that contribute to fine living.

Prior to the 1970s it was imprudent for a woman to indicate her interest in a man, nowadays that's quite acceptable provided it is done with decorum, a change but not without order. We have a charge to keep the legacy that we received; similarly, we are required to provide a legacy for future generations.

*Protocol is an interesting cyclical process; it is inescapable and all-inclusive; protocol is the universal modus operandi. PROTOCOL therefore, should not be misconstrued as formality.*

## Corporate

In the corporate arena protocols vary as institutions differ relative to marketing strategies. In the diplomatic services, there are set guidelines for addressing dignitaries. In the military services there is no room for confusion, the protocol is well established and rigidly observed. In an office one-on-one a boss might be Bill or Ana; however, when we speak of the boss with a stranger; or if we need to call from afar; he/she is unequivocally, Mr. Smith, Ms. Smith or Dr. Smith.

Set protocols have always existed for recruiting health care providers. Recently however, to embrace the prevailing shortage of qualified nurses, the policies and procedures were revised. Generally, such revisions do eliminate a few ethical requirements. Conversely, the missing behavioral codes still exist but in the new order they provide the "preference edge" within the final selection process.

In the legal system, the way we present ourselves and the way an attorney presents a case are key to whether we win or lose. When we fail to engage competent representation, we lose the opportunity before losing the case. Our action then compares with the mythical man who worked all of his life, acquired much and stored all of his possessions in a shed but failed to provide reliable security because, he said, "Proper locks cost much in dollars, way beyond my means to purchase."

Let us compare and contrast simple career damage as opposed to career advancement. The Vice President of a company asks an assistant to collect some documents that belong to the CEO; on his return from the errand the assistant crosses paths with the CEO and hands over the papers. An employee who knows how to further his career would be cognizant of the fact that a more refined behavioral pattern would impress the corporate executives positively and thereby contribute to his advancement. The hidden message in this scenario is the way that humility maintains a strategic position as it does in most other facets of the circle of life.

Although we do not always consciously make the effort, it is clear that everything we do follows a certain path in the implementation of behaviors that improve our effectiveness as we utilize life's basic ethical norms as our road map.

# Live YOUR Dream

*"A rock pile ceases to be a rock pile the moment
a single dreamer contemplates it, bearing within him
the image of a cathedral"*
~ Antoine de Saint-Exupery

Everyone has a dream. They come in all sizes and different degrees of daring. But each person has some wish they would like to see come true. You may wish it as you blow out the candles on your birthday cake ~ you may wish it as you toss a coin into a fountain ~ or you may wish it as you see a blazing star flashing downward from the heavens, striking its path across the sky.

You may tell the world about your dream or keep it a secret, whispering it only to heaven in your prayers. But bringing a dream to life involves much more than dreaming. It involves weeping, working, struggling and holding fast to the dream through whatever may come. Your dream is your purpose for living. It is incentive, encouragement, and reason to be, all rolled into one.

You are endowed with the ability to create for yourself any life of which you believe yourself capable. If you are a bricklayer, act as though it is your own life being constructed with every brick that you lay. If you are a seamstress, leave not one seam unfinished - nor one thread uncut. It is the fabric of your existence with which you are creating, not just the material in your fingers.

If you form a mental picture of your dream and turn away in disbelief every time you envision your desire, your energy works in reverse. So use the technique of thought substitution to clean up any negative visions that may arise. Raise your mental sights gradually to accommodate your capacity to believe, for you must believe what you see before the power can be activated.

Miracles are the gifts of the dreamers to the world. You make the difference between the possible and the impossible, between the dream and the reality. Cherish your dreams. Desire them with all your heart. Believe in them and work to make them come true.

# Visions and Ideals

### From the Classic: *As a Man Thinketh*

### by James Allen

The dreamers are the saviors of the world. As the visible world is sustained by the invisible, so men, through all their trials and sins and sordid vocations, are nourished by the beautiful visions of their solitary dreamers. Humanity cannot forget its dreamers; it cannot let their ideals fade and die; it lives in them; it knows them, as the realities which it shall one day see and know. Composer, sculptor, painter, poet, prophet, sage, these are the makers of the after world, the architects of heaven. The world is beautiful because they have lived, without them, laboring humanity would perish.

He who cherishes a beautiful vision, a lofty ideal in his heart, will one day realize it. Columbus cherished a vision of another world, and he discovered it; Copernicus fostered the vision of a spiritual world of stainless beauty and perfect peace, and he entered into it.

Cherish your visions; cherish your ideals; cherish the music that stirs in your heart, the beauty that forms in your mind, the loveliness that drapes your purest thoughts, for out of them will grow all delightful conditions, all heavenly environment; of these, if you but remain true to them, your world will at last be built.

Dream lofty dreams, and as you dream, so you shall become. Your Vision is the promise of what you shall one day be; your Ideal is the prophecy of what you shall at last unveil.

The greatest achievement at first and for a time is a dream. The oak sleeps in the acorn; the bird waits in the egg; and in the highest vision of the soul a waking angel stirs. Dreams are the seedlings of realities.

Your circumstances may be uncongenial, but they shall not long remain so if you but perceive an Ideal and strive for it. You cannot travel within and stand still without. Here is a youth hard pressed by poverty and labor, confined long hours in an unhealthy workshop unschooled, and lacking all the arts of refinement. But he dreams of better things; he thinks of intelligence, refinement, of grace and beauty. He conceives of, mentally builds up, an ideal condition of life, the vision of a wider liberty and a larger scope takes possession of him; unrest urges him to action and he utilizes all his spare time and means, small though they are, to the development of his latent powers and resources. Very soon so altered has his mind become that the workshop can no longer hold him. It has become so out of harmony with his mentality that it falls out of his life as a garment is cast aside, and, with the growth of opportunities, which fit the scope of his expanding powers, he passes out of it forever. Years later we see this youth as a full-grown man. We find him a master of certain forces of the mind, which he wields with worldwide influence and almost unequaled power. In his hands he holds the chords of gigantic responsibilities, he speaks, and lo! Lives are changed; men and women hang upon his words and remold their characters, and sunlike, he becomes the fixed and luminous center round which innumerable destinies evolve. He has realized the Vision of his youth. He has become one with his Ideal.

*Into your hands will be placed the exact results of your own thoughts; and you will receive that which you earn, no more, no less. Whatever your present environment may be, you will fall, remain, or rise with your thoughts, your Vision, your Ideal.*

And you, too, youthful reader, will realize the Vision (not the idle wish) of your heart, be it base or beautiful, or a mixture of both, for you will always gravitate toward that which you, secretly, most love. Into your hands will be placed the exact results of your own thoughts; and you will receive that which you earn, no more, no less. Whatever your present environment may be, you will fall, remain, or rise with your thoughts, your Vision, your Ideal. You will become as small as your controlling desire; as great as your dominant aspiration; in the beautiful words of Stanton Kirkham Davis, "You may be keeping accounts, and presently you shall walk out of the door that for so long as seemed to you the barrier of your ideals, and shall find yourself before an audience – the pen still behind your ear, the ink stains on your fingers – and then there shall pour out the torrent of your inspiration. You may be driving sheep, and you shall wander to the city – bucolic and opened-mouthed; shall wander under the intrepid guidance of the spirit into the studio of the master, and after a time he shall say, " I have nothing more to teach you." And now you have become the master, who did so recently dream of great things while driving sheep. You shall lay down the saw and the plane to take upon yourself the generation of the world."

The thoughtless, the ignorant, and the indolent, seeing only the apparent effects of things and not the things themselves, talk of luck, of fortune, and chance. Seeing a man grow rich, they say, "How lucky he is!" Observing another become intellectual, they exclaim, "How highly favored he is!" And noting the sacred character and wide influence of another, they remark, "How chance aids him at every turn!" They do not see the trials and failures and struggles which these men have voluntarily encountered in order to gain their experience; have no knowledge of the sacrifices they have made, of the undaunted efforts they have put forth, of the faith they have exercised, that they might overcome the apparently insurmountable; and realize the Vision of their heart. They do not know the darkness and the heartaches; they only see the light and joy, and call it "luck", do not see the long and arduous journey, but only behold the pleasant goal, and call it "good fortune"; do not understand the process, but only perceive the result, and call it "chance".

In all human affairs there are efforts, and there are results, and the strength of the effort is the measure of the result. Chance is not "Gifts," powers, material, intellectual, and spiritual possessions are the fruits of effort; they are thoughts completed, objects accomplished, visions realized.

---

*The Visions that you glorify in your mind,*
*the Ideal that you enthrone in your heart –*
*this you will build your life by,*
*this you will become*

---

# DAVE LINIGER, CHAIRMAN OF THE BOARD
## CO-FOUNDER OF RE/MAX INTERNATIONAL, INC.

**Dave Liniger's** success is rooted in the most precious possession of American citizenship: *the invincible power of each individual to create his or her own destiny.* Dave's faith, his desire, his imagination, and his persistence were the ingredients for the creation and legendary success of industry giant RE/MAX International, Inc. RE/MAX, at its essence, is a worldwide franchise network, now in its third decade of consecutive growth, with more than 84,000 top-notch Real Estate Professionals --- who join him in furthering a wide variety of worthy causes nation-wide.

When Dave started RE/MAX over 30 years ago, he was a struggling real estate agent with the all-consuming dream of creating a new kind of real estate organization - one that truly recognized and rewarded its top producers. He worked around the clock to attract the *doers* with the inner resources to make things happen. With dogged determination he would overcome every obstacle to build one of the worlds' most successful real estate organizations through leadership and team building. He is generally credited with doing more than anyone in the industry to improve the working conditions and income potential of sales agents.

Liniger is nationally recognized as an expert in time management, sales training, motivation, and recruiting. He has been featured in *Entrepreneur, Forbes, Fortune, Inc., Success* and other leading publications and has appeared extensively on television and radio throughout North America. Liniger has been inducted into the Council of Real Estate Brokerage Managers (CRB) Hall of Leaders and the REBAC (ABR) Hall of Fame.

Like most self-made men, Dave Liniger likes to reminisce. He credits his Midwestern roots for instilling the bedrock values of discipline, honesty, the work ethic and self-reliance. Born in Marion, Indiana, he was the eldest and adopted son of a successful small town businessman. Growing up on his family's 40-acre farm, almost a decade older than his two sisters and one brother, he developed a sense of responsibility at an early age.

Smart and hard working, with a tremendous amount of potential, Dave nevertheless did not find his challenge or sense of purpose in school. He dropped out of the University of Indiana, married his high school sweetheart and soon joined the military, seeing action in Vietnam. Returning to the states after the war, he soon found that the $99 a month paid to entry-level airmen did not support a growing family. Therefore, Dave supplemented his military position with three part-time jobs, rising at 2 am to begin an exhausting round of delivering papers, performing his airman duties, working at a filling station daily and in a theater on weekends.

### 'The Die Was Cast'

All the while Dave yearned to balance his need to be economically productive with his need to find an outlet for his relentless desire to make his mark. As a teenager, he had read *Think & Grow Rich* by Napoleon Hill and was strongly influenced by its message: *"Whatever the Mind of Man Can Conceive and Believe, It Can Achieve"*. He was ripe for creative ideas when he read a book by a postman who took a thousand dollars, invested it in a distressed property, and turned it into a real estate fortune. Armed with the knowledge and the principles laid out in that book he decided to take some of his own hard-earned money and buy his first property in Tucson, Arizona. When he sold it one year later for a $4000 profit—more than his combined pay from the military and three part-time jobs—"The die was cast," as he tells it today.

Dave continued his military career while buying and selling investment properties. Ever conscious of the next opportunity, he began to think 'If I am going to be a real estate investor, I should save the commissions and get a real estate license."

He had no intention of ever becoming a real estate agent. "I was shy, a farm boy," he said. "Even though I was in my twenties, I looked twelve." But, he did get licensed and soon decided to try selling other properties to earn commissions.

"The first six months I was a disaster," he said. "There I was in Phoenix, trying to sell houses in the middle of the summer in a Volkswagen with no air conditioning. I had this inferiority complex because I looked so young for my age and everyone I talked to was not only older, but knew more about real estate than me. I had no confidence at all. I was ready to give up." He was at a critical crossroad. Dave had prepaid $25 for an all day seminar by the famous real estate motivational speaker, Dave Stone. The encounter changed his life forever.

"I sat in the front row and got so pumped up by the man's confidence and smooth delivery, I kept jumping up throughout the seminar, shouting, 'Mr. Stone, I want to be like you!'" said Dave. "I was convinced if I could do it the way he did it, I'd be a success too! Right then I chose him to be my mentor. I bought all of his books and tapes. Wherever and whenever he spoke, I was in the front row. And every day, I read and absorbed the positive messages, which were of great importance to me. They helped stimulate my thinking and instilled in me the knowledge that you could do anything just as soon as you believe that you can.

*All the powers go to work for you*
*as soon as that belief takes root*
*and nothing becomes impossible."*

### The First Sale

**"The power of that attitude start working for me that very night.** On the way home I stopped at a convenience store and standing next to me at the checkout counter was a cute little Hispanic girl, about 18 years old, talking to her father. I got the sense they were talking about selling or buying a house. Pumped with sudden confidence, I approached her, *'Excuse me, Miss, I'm a Realtor and I can help you.'* She said her father wanted to move from Phoenix to Albuquerque and needed to sell his house, but couldn't speak English. He didn't speak English and I didn't speak Spanish, so with her as the interpreter, I listed the property right there. It was a little fix-up property in vogue back in the 60's. I stayed up all night and moved it the next morning. It made me feel great that I could do this for them and they were so happy that they referred me to another Hispanic family. . .who referred me to another. . .who referred me to another. In two days, I had gone from no sale or listing in six months to four listings and four sales in less than 48 hours. It was exhilarating! I wasn't the most experienced person, but I sure would work around the clock. And I really cared about my customers." explained Dave.

"The confidence and energy that came after the first few sales was *up above the crowd.* 'Wow! I can do this.' I'd get up at five in the morning and drive the streets so I would know all the neighborhoods. I just outworked everybody and it paid off. I became incredibly good at selling. And, of course, I really liked the money I was bringing in. But one thing kept bothering me. It was my hard work, not the company that I was working for, that created the sales. I was the one getting up at 5 in the morning, knocking on doors, giving up my evenings and week-ends, putting up signs, taking care of my customers. *Why should I give half of everything that resulted from my hard work to the company?"*

# GAIL LINIGER

# THE FIRST LADY OF RE/MAX

**Gail Liniger,** RE/MAX Co-Founder and Vice Chairman of the Board, is an extraordinary woman. She earned her reputation as an astute industry leader through a great amount of talent and know-how, a strong positive attitude and a determination to succeed. On a more personal level, her almost miraculous recovery from a near-fatal crash of a small private airplane in 1983 has served to inspire and motivate people both inside and outside the RE/MAX organization.

Born in St. Louis, Missouri, Gail received her marketing degree from Southern Illinois University. In 1973 she moved to Denver and became the first employee to join RE/MAX. Gail was elected Vice President within the year. Along the way, she received countless state and national awards including Colorado's *"Entrepreneur of the Year"* by *Ernest & Young*, and *Inc. Magazine*. From a field of nearly 8,000 participants nationally, she was named first-runner-up.

An avid-golfer, most people who see her for the first time are amazed that she even plays the game. A brace on her left leg assists her in walking and one arm is immobile, while her left side vision is restricted – all a result of the accident. But those who know how tenacious Gail is are thrilled but not surprised that she recently executed 'golf's hardest feat' a Hole-in-One!

Gail Liniger's winning spirit is the basis of a life lived with hopefulness and meaning. Patron of the Arts, champion of worthy causes, devoted to her family and the business she loves, she is acknowledged as one of the industry's most inspirational leaders.

## The Move to Denver, Colorado

After finishing his time in the military, Dave was drawn to Denver by his love of the mountain life—hunting, fishing and camping. His reputation as one of the best real estate salespeople in Arizona would follow him. He chose to work for market leaders in the real estate industry, but began to conceptualize innovations he would implement if he ran his own business. His instincts for the direction the real estate industry should move focused on a radically new set of ideas. The sales people would have an entrepreneurial stake. "We all risk together and we all benefit together. I knew it was key. We introduced the concept to top salespeople and the response was overwhelmingly positive. We believed in our company and we believed in each other."

## The Beginning of a Winning Partnership

The first RE/MAX employee Dave hired in Denver was Gail Main. While Dave excelled at sales, training, motivation and recruiting, Gail put her college background and expertise in business management to work opening offices and organizing the accounting, financial and legal aspects of the new company. She would become profoundly important to the success of RE/MAX and to Dave himself.

Gail's combination of skill and savvy kept the business afloat when the recession of 1973 hit Denver hard, drying up most of RE/MAX's financial backing. His Midwest perseverance again carrying him through, Dave vowed that he would survive the economic downturn and pay back all he owed. "I guaranteed every creditor I would not file bankruptcy. I kept my word and paid back every dime we owed anyone. But the negative publicity was awful.

*Like every adversity in life,*
*if you get through it,*
*you get stronger."*

81

Gail recognized, however, that Dave was using up most of his energy managing the financial crisis, squeezing in sales and training as he could. "'You're wasting your time,' she told me," Dave said. "'You hire salespeople and I will deal with the creditors.' Since we were upside down and losing money, I worked eighteen hours a day selling and the rest of the time recruiting and training. But Gail was the one who negotiated the financial mess we were in. It worked."

Dave & Gail's partnership blossomed and they married ten years after opening the first RE/MAX office. It is the foundation upon which one of the nation's largest and most successful real estate network was built.

## Winners Attract Winners

With definiteness of purpose, Dave set out to attract the best salespeople he could find in the hyper-competitive world of real estate sales. And he would shake up the industry by offering a new idea into the mix. He offered top producers maximum compensation and the freedom to conduct their own business within a corporate framework that would in time be instantly credible to the consumer.

"I knew from my own experience what a leap of faith salespeople make. Salespeople are not conformists. They are risk-takers willing to gamble on their own ability and talent. Their well being and that of their families rely on their ability to produce. No one is keeping score but themselves. They know the harder they work, the luckier they get. They believe in themselves. Why else would anyone choose a profession without a guaranteed income, where success is measured on a daily basis? Sometimes things get difficult. The voice of the critics will come from all directions. You get tested. *And the test is not whether you can; the test is whether you will.* When anyone is willing to take a risk, to put his or her all on the line, losing is not possible. For a person who is not suited, that can be frightening because there's nobody there to direct you or write you a check. However, for those who are ready, for those who are entrepreneurs at heart, the value of freedom and independence is the motivator."

## Women Enter the Market

"In the 1950's, the industry was totally dominated by gray-haired men in flannel suits. I didn't yet have name awareness, or market share to convince the top producers to make the leap 'If you ever become successful, let me know. I'll join you' was the usual response. But a really interesting aspect is that, at that time, only about 2% of sales agents were women. We knew women would be a natural in this business. They are great listeners and connect easily on a personal level. So, we started hiring and training homemakers and single moms who wanted an extra income, but needed flexible hours. They loved the whole process of helping people find the home of their dreams and they succeeded even beyond expectations. Women became, and are to this day, a vital part of the RE/MAX success story."

## Outstanding Agents. Outstanding Results

Even in the midst of a financial downtown, 21 REMAX agents achieved $33 million in home sales the first year in business. To counteract negative publicity over its financing troubles, and relentless criticism from the established real estate companies upset with the new kids in town, RE/MAX agents bought a full-page newspaper ad that year, and on each succeeding anniversary, picturing the entire sales force and office staff and touting their steady success. The second year agents grew to 41, the third 134, and the fifth 289.

"When sales hit a billion in the sixth year and the ad had grown to eight pages to fit in hundreds of agents, we were all so excited about it! The pages were laid out in front of us with this headline *"A BILLION SOLD!"* Everyone approved it except Dean Gattis, my friend and a leading franchise manager. He insisted instead of trumpeting sales, the staff should run the ad with the headline: "We would like to thank the 39,381 Colorado families who entrusted their business to RE/MAX." Gattis pointed out that RE/MAX agents live side-by-side with their customers in the same communities. They share the same joys and struggles of the families they serve and those families by choosing RE/MAX, sometimes more than once, were supporting our families and us. *"We need to thank them."*

## RE/MAX Community Involvement

*RE/MAX Associates have always been among the leaders in their communities, devoting time, effort and dollars to countless local causes and far-reaching charities. They conduct fund-raisers and work as volunteers to benefit youth, the needy and others. Associates' contributions build their community presence – and ultimately, a network-wide image of citizenship.*

*The Craig Hospital:* Among the many organizations that annually receive whole-hearted support from Dave and Gail Liniger, probably the one nearest to their hearts is Craig Hospital in Denver. The caring, expert staff at Craig was instrumental in Gail's recovery from a near-fatal small airplane crash in 1983. Both Gail and Dave—who remained at his then-to-be wife's side every day of her recuperation—are forever grateful for the compassion they experienced at Craig.

*Children's Miracle Network:* Since RE/MAX became the organization's exclusive real estate sponsor in 1992; RE/MAX associates have raised more than $40 million for the charity. The nonprofit organization's 170 participating hospitals across North America help 17 million children annually.

*Susan G. Komen Breast Cancer Foundation:* With its "RE/MAX Racing for Life" slogan, RE/MAX is proud to be a co-sponsor of the National Series Breast Cancer Survivor Recognition Program at the Komen Race for the Cure events. Corporate representatives solicit fund-raising pledges and host Breast Cancer Survivor Recognition tents at the races.

*Sanctuary Golf Course:* Besides RE/MAX Associates, Dave and Gail Liniger give back to the community, notably by making their nationally renowned private golf course, available to charities for fund-raising golf tournaments. Ninety-eight charity tournaments have raised more than $14 million since the course opened in 1997.

*The Wildlife Experience:* RE/MAX International is the first major sponsor of this conservation and community center promoting understanding of the natural world and its conservation through art and education.

## Premier Community Citizenship

"At that moment it all came together for me. Gattis was right. We changed the whole company philosophy from stating that we are the top producers to *recognizing the people in our communities who make our success possible.* We began focusing on the fact that we are all alike, we are all struggling to find our own place in the American dream. We began putting great importance on making a difference not only in our own lives, but in the lives of others as well. We changed the RE/MAX ads to reflect that approach and set the company on the road to a more heightened awareness of the role that corporations play in the communities they serve. *And, I knew that when we dedicate ourselves to a purpose that will enrich the lives of others, and work toward the fulfillment of that purpose, the rewards will come.*"

## Premier Market Share

The scope and influence RE/MAX has in the global market began with the vision, hard work and persistence of a man who never forgets that he did not build RE/MAX alone. "All of our best ideas came from our team, including our Hot Air Balloon Logo, which was the brainchild of Bill Echols, now our Vice President of Public Relations." Dave says. "We have many people to thank. *It was always a team effort.*"

The interaction of quality Associates, public recognition of the RE/MAX name and logo, customer satisfaction and Associate citizenship results in transactions and leading market share. That market share – similar in effect to the original RE/MAX maximum commission concept – attracts more top producers, who perpetuate the cycle of business success.

Yes, Dave Liniger is a leader who shaped his own destiny by motivating and inspiring others to do the same. *What we believe we become.* When we recognize that this is the right of all Americans, we become the empowered people that make up the strength, and hope, of this nation.

# Be Persistent

You don't have to hit it hard ~ just be persistent
Make certain that you hit it every day.
Repeated pressure, steady and insistent
Like drops of water wears the stone away.
You don't have to move the mountain right this minute,
With a single surge of struggle, stretch and strain;
Bit by bit, remove the earth within it,
One day your mountain will become a plain.
You don't have to grab a star in one swift motion,
Just press on every day from where you are.
Keep your faith, and don't give up the notion,
It's possible for you to reach your star.
A million drops of water in the ocean,
Doesn't stop a ship from setting sail;
A soul in quest must stay in constant motion,
Until its jet propelled along the trail.
Progress is not a capsule that you swallow.
Nor a chance affair along the way.
Work, persist ~ success will surely follow.
Don't hit it hard! Just hit it every day!

© Pat Sampson

# SALESPEOPLE

*You are Salespeople!*
*A rare and wonderful breed*
*Ranging from sea to sea.*
*Inspiring, appealing, succeeding;*
*Yet different as different can be.*
*A bread-and-butter-and-blood vignette*
*Is the life you salespeople live.*
*The bread-and-butter is what you get.*
*The blood is what you give!*
*With humor in heart ~*
*Briefcase in hand*
*You trek the track of your trade.*
*Planets apart from common man*
*From super star stuff you're made!*
*Your love of life is a grand romance,*
*Every scene a rose colored sight.*
*You laugh at luck, you chuckle at chance.*
*You give bad breaks a fight!*
*Every day you wend your way ~*
*Your ego on the line.*
*You're a positive thinking protégé*
*You're always super fine!*
*You give it your guts*
*You dare to excel*
*You play poker with the gods.*
*You don't hear 'buts'*
*You weave a spell.*
*You dare to upset the odds!*
*When you say you're a salesperson,*
*Don't say it like a true confession.*
*Stand straight! Walk tall!*
*Make a sale, man!*
*You're part of a noble profession!*

© Pat Sampson

# BRIAN TRACY

**Brian Tracy** is Chairman and CEO of Brian Tracy International, a human resources company specializing in the training and development of individuals and organizations.

Brian is the best-selling author of more than 30 books, and has written and produced more than 300 audio and video learning programs, including the worldwide, best-selling *Psychology of Achievement,* which has been translated into more than 20 languages. Brian addresses more than 250,000 people each year, addressing audiences as large as 20,000 people. He has spoken in 24 countries. He speaks four languages.

He speaks to corporate and public audiences on the subjects of personal and professional development, including the executives and staff of many of America's largest corporations. He has conducted high level consulting assignments with several billion-dollar plus corporations in strategic planning and organizational development.

Brian Tracy's exciting talks and seminars on Leadership, Selling, Self-Esteem, Goals, Strategy, Creativity and Success Psychology bring about immediate changes and long-term results.

*The Seven Secrets of Success* are excerpted from Brian Tracy's book, *Be A Sales Superstar*, published by Berrett-Koehle

Write Brian Tracy International,
462 Stevens Avenue, Suite 202,
Solana Beach, California 92075
or visit his website: *www.briantracy.com*

There are seven secrets, or principles, of sales success. They are practiced by all the highest paid salespeople every day. The regular application of these principles is virtually guaranteed to move you to the top of your field.

## Secret One

Get serious! Make a decision to go all the way to the top of your field. Make a today decision to join the top 10%. There is no one and nothing that can hold you back from being the best except yourself. Remember, it takes just as long to be great as to be mediocre. The time is going to pass anyway. Your job is to commit to excellence, to get better and better each day, and to never, never stop until you reach the summit.

## Secret Two

Identify your limiting skill to sales success. Identify your weakest single skill and make a plan to become absolutely excellent in that area. Ask yourself, and your boss, *"What one skill, if I developed and did it consistently in an excellent fashion, would have the greatest positive impact on my sales?"* Whatever your answer to this question, write it down, set a deadline, make a plan, and then work on it every day. This decision alone can change your life.

## Secret Three

Get around the right people. Get around positive, successful people. Associate with men and women who are going somewhere with their lives. And get away from negative, critical, complaining people. They drag you down, tire you out, distract and discourage you, and lead you inevitably to underachievement and failure. Remember, you cannot fly with the eagles if you continue to scratch with the turkeys.

## SECRET FOUR

Take excellent care of your physical health. You need high levels of energy to sell effectively, and to bounce back from continual rejection and discouragement. Be sure to eat the right foods, get the right amount of exercise and get plenty of rest and recreation. Make a decision that you are going to live to be 80 years old, or more, and begin today to do whatever you have to do to achieve that goal.

## SECRET FIVE

Visualize yourself as one of the top people in your field. Imagine yourself performing at your best all day long. Feed your subconscious mind with vivid, exciting, emotionalized pictures of yourself as positive, confident, competent and completely in control of every part of your life. These clear mental pictures preprogram you and motivate you to sell at your best in any situation.

## SECRET SIX

Practice positive self-talk continually. Control your inner dialogue. Talk to yourself the way you want to be rather than the way you might be today. For example, repeat to yourself these powerful words, over and over again. *"I like myself! I'm the best! I can do it! I love my work!"* Say to yourself, *"I feel happy! I feel healthy! I feel terrific!"*

Remember, fully 95% of your emotions are determined by the way you talk to yourself, most of the time. The way you feel determines how you behave. And how you behave determines how much you sell.

Your job is to get yourself on an upward spiral where you think and talk to yourself positively, all day long. You think, walk, talk and act like the very best people in your field. When you do, your success becomes inevitable.

# SECRET SEVEN

Take positive action toward your goals, every single day. Be proactive rather than reactive. Grab the bull by the horns. If you are not happy with your income, get out there and get face to face with more customers. If you are not happy with any part of your life, accept responsibility and take charge.

All successful salespeople are intensely action oriented. They have a sense of urgency. They develop a bias for action. They do it now! They have a compulsion to closure. They maintain a fast tempo and move quickly in everything they do.

*And the good news is this.* The faster you move, the more energy you have. The faster you move, the more ground you cover. The faster you move, the more people you see. The more people you see, the more experience you get. The more experience you get, the more sales you make. The more people you see and the more sales you make, the more your self-esteem and self respect goes up, and the more you will feel like great about yourself. You will have more energy. You will be happier and more positive.

The faster you move, the more you take complete control of your entire life and virtually guarantee that you will be one of the top performers and the highest paid people in your field.

*Salespeople are among the most important people in America.* Every single company depends for its survival on the success of its salespeople. High sales is the number one reason for company success. Low sales is the number one reason for company failure. And you can be in the driver's seat.

The choice is up to you. No genuine effort is ever lost. You can reach for the stars in your sales career if you are willing to set exciting goals for yourself and then go to work to make your dreams come true.

# CHRISTOPHER BROWN

**Christopher Brown** is a man of great energy, wit and enthusiasm, who practices a positive philosophy in every area of his life. Chris grew up in a home with eight siblings, is deeply committed to family and remains close with his parents, who have been and continue to be a guiding light of inspiration to him. Graduating from college with a degree in Physics and Mathematics, he pursued an engineering career and spent fifteen years as a transportation safety consultant. As time went on, he realized that because of his strong connection with others he wanted to branch off into a business that involved direct connection and involvement with people. Despite the daunting nature of changing careers, Chris had the courage and strength to let go of the comfortable and familiar and embark on a major life change. Entering the field of real estate sales in the Washington DC metro area, where he grew up, proved to be a great choice. In a relatively short period of time, he reached the status of a multi-million dollar producer in the respected Long and Foster Real Estate firm. Although committed and dedicated to helping families find the home of their dreams, his love of learning and technology motivates him to tutor students of all education levels whenever his schedule allows. "I get a real lift out of helping young people realize their potential. Knowing that today, like yesterday, and tomorrow, we all have the opportunity in a free society to make the most of ourselves, to be our best, and realize our dreams."

Christopher Brown, Realtor®
Long and Foster Inc.
Potomac, Maryland Branch
301-928-2479 Mobile Phone
*Chris.Brown@longandfoster.com* E-mail

*"Treat a person as he is, and he will remain as he is.
Treat him as he could be, and he will become what he should be."*

~ Jimmy Johnson

Everyone is a salesperson. We all make sales every day. We use our power of persuasion to convince others to respond to us in some way. When we think of life that way, it gives us a chance to think about how we want to approach others, not just in business but in our every action and deed.

So what are some of the fundamental guidelines for getting your customer's interest? Those who believe in the value of their services and products share the opportunity with as many people as possible. By helping others to improve the quality of their lives and get what they want, you are naturally going to thrive and flourish.

A lot of people think that packaging is what's important and there's some truth in that - a good package never hurts. In the long term, though, it is what's inside the package that really matters.

Are you kind and thoughtful? Do you put yourself into the other person's place so you are aware not only of your own needs but theirs as well? Do you treat them the way you yourself want to be treated? Do you care about making them comfortable? Do you know how to listen and think about what is being said to you?

Do you pay attention to life? There is nothing that happens to us, including our mistakes, from which we don't learn something. Recognize this, and there are no bad days, there are only rich learning experiences which deepen us as human beings.

Do you have passion and humor? Passion, a vision, something you care about, gives your life meaning and purpose. It makes you interesting to yourself and therefore interesting to others. And then there is humor. Humor is one of the greatest gifts we have in life. Nothing is more contagious than laughter or more healing and sustaining. Research has shown that even pretending to smile – putting your muscles into the smile position – changes your body chemistry. A smile is one of the most powerful treasures we have in life. It's worth its weight in gold and the more you share it, the more it multiplies. Now's the time to live it and share it!

# Paul McGhee, Ph.D

**Paul McGhee,** president of The Laughter Remedy in Wilmington, Delaware, has been featured in The New York Times, USA Today, The Learning Channel, PBS, and numerous European magazines and newspapers and television shows. He has conducted humor programs for the AICPA, General Motors, Xerox, AT&T, Merck, Pfizer, MetLife, Prudential, Merrill-Lynch and many other Fortune 500 companies. He has written 12 books on humor and writes columns about its health benefits at his website, www.LaughterRemedy.com.. Order Dr. McGhee's latest book, *Health, Healing, and the Amuse System: Humor as Survival Training* by calling 800-228-0810.

# Humor is FUNdamental to Positive Living and Helps You Cope with Stress

Stress has become as American as apple pie. We have steadily mounting stress from our jobs, relationships, health care costs, threats of terrorism, and on and on. In order to remain effective on the job, hold your marriage together, and keep your sanity, you have no choice but to become more resilient. And your sense of humor is one of the most powerful tools you have to help you remain emotionally resilient on the tough days.

Stress interferes with job performance by producing an emotional state (anger, anxiety, or depression) that keeps you from staying focused on the task at hand. When you find or create something funny in the midst of your upset, it quickly substitutes a frame of mind that is incompatible with these negative emotions. It enables you to "let go" of the upset caused by stress.

If you've ever had the experience of laughing at something while you were really upset, what happened to the upset? It weakened, right? It's hard to hang on to your anger when you are laughing. So humor works, in part, by substituting a positive for a negative frame of mind. When you improve your humor skills, it gives you a means of taking control over your mood – even in the midst of stress – enabling you to maintain a frame of mind conducive to functioning at peak levels.

Researchers concur that the ability to manage one's emotions, as well as the emotions of others, is one of the most crucial components of emotional intelligence--a form of intelligence now considered crucial to corporate success. And humor is one of the most powerful tools you have to help manage your emotions on a day-to-day basis.

A sense of humor also helps keep problems in perspective. A good laugh makes it easier to see that "this too will pass." Finally, most people report that high stress saps their energy as the day goes on, leaving them drained and eager to quit for the day. Humor and laughter have the power to turn this around and actually increase your energy level. This goes a long way in fighting burnout on the job.

Research has also shown that laughter reduces muscle tension. This muscle relaxation, and the easing of psychological tension that goes with it, is the main goal of all stress management techniques, and clearly accounts for much of the stress-reducing power of humor.

So humor and laughter have much more power to sustain a positive frame of body, mind and spirit than you probably ever imagined. But even if a good daily dose of laughter doesn't add years to your life, it will certainly add life to your years.

To get this positive influence of humor into your own life, start looking for the light side of everyday situations and observe what this does to your daily mood. You soon have more and more experiences like I had at my local supermarket recently. With a long line of people waiting behind me as I took my Mastercard out to pay for my groceries, I discovered that the credit card swiping machine had been changed since my previous visit. I hesitated several seconds trying to figure out how to hold the card, and which button to press first. The cashier got impatient and said to me, "Strip down and face toward me." I slowly looked at her and said, "Are you sure you want me to do that?" Her reaction was embarrassment, but it made my day!

Remember, *they who laugh, last.*

# Fun with Mark Twain

- Often it does seem a pity that Noah and his party did not miss the boat.

- Often a hen who has merely laid an egg cackles as if she has laid an asteroid.

- It is better to keep your mouth shut and appear stupid
  than to open it and remove all doubt.

- It is noble to be good; it is still nobler to teach others to be good -
  and less trouble.

- Let your secret sympathies and your compassion be always with the under
  dog in the fight - this is magnanimity; but bet on the other one -
  this is business.

- Good friends, good books and a sleepy conscience: this is the ideal life.

- Denial ain't just a river in Egypt.

- Under certain circumstances, profanity provides a relief
  denied even to prayer.

- Go to Heaven for the climate, Hell for the company.

- Sacred cows make the best hamburger.

- To cease smoking is the easiest thing I ever did.
  I ought to know, I've done it a thousand times.

- When I was a boy of 14, my father was so ignorant I could hardly stand
  to have the old man around. But when I got to be 21, I was astonished at
  how much the old man had learned in seven years.

- Always do right. This will gratify some people and astonish the rest.

- A banker is a fellow who lends you his umbrella when the sun is shining, but wants it back the minute it begins to rain.

- Always acknowledge a fault. This will throw those in authority off their guard and give you an opportunity to commit more.

- Be careful about reading health books. You may die of a misprint.

- Clothes make the man. Naked people have little or no influence on society.

- Few things are harder to put up with than the annoyance of a good example.

- The report of my death was an exaggeration.

- There are several good protections against temptation, but the surest is cowardice.

- The rule is perfect: in all matters of opinion our adversaries are insane.

- Familiarity breeds contempt – and children.

- Never put off until tomorrow what you can do the day after tomorrow.

- Water in moderation cannot hurt anybody.

- I have never let my schooling interfere with my education.

- I thoroughly disapprove of duels. If a man should challenge me, I would take him kindly and forgivingly by the hand and lead him to a quiet place and kill him.

- I don't give a damn for a man who can only spell a word one way.

- I am opposed to millionaires, but it would be dangerous to offer me the position.

- Whenever you find yourself on the side of the many, it is time to reform.

- By trying we can easily learn to endure adversity. Another man's, I mean.

- It takes your enemy and your friend, working together to hurt you: the one to slander you, and the other to get the news to you.

- Get your facts first, and then you can distort them as much as you please.

- Honesty is the best policy, where there is money in it.

- Humor is the great thing, the saving thing. The minute it comes up, all our irritations and resentments slip away, and a sunny spirit takes its place.

# Rock and A Hard Place

'Tween a Rock and a Hard Place, here I be,
The whole darn world's crashing in on me.
Though I'm tightly pressed in this most precarious place,
I'm making the best of my limited working space.
I'm thinking of producing a fossil of my face!

You've got to work with what you've got, right within your clutch,
I always give it my greatest shot when I haven't got too much.
Of course, I'm not recommending you get into a hole,
Though poets say adversity steels the tender soul.
I must be steeled completely, for it always seems to be,
The space 'tween a rock and a hard place
Is invariably stuffed with me!

At dawn I carefully chart my course, by afternoon I've strayed.
By evening I've quite forgotten the careful plans I've made.
It's not that everything goes wrong,
That's putting matters a little strong.
But there are moments among my days
Would drive a saint to wicked ways!

Now you don't mess around, but now and then slip,
Take a contraband friend for a friendly little nip.
Somewhere between the wine and the slaw,
You look dead into the eyes of your mother-in-law.
And all you want to do is to hide your face,
'Tween your rock and your hard, hard place!

Like the time you were skating and took a spill,
Rolled to the bottom of the long, long hill.
Your friends all laughed and your heart stood still.
You were 'twixt and 'tween a cattle stampede
and an eight-lane highway you didn't need.
A Mack Truck's approaching with all due speed.
You're in a hard place and glad to be in it.
Things look like they'll be worse in a minute!

Just keep believing that life is sweet,
Stoically receiving the bitter and sweet.
Keep a song in your heart - a smile on your face,
You'll immortalize your Rock,
and your Hard, Hard Place!

© Pat Sampson

# Life's Funny with Money

*"I don't make deals for the money. I've got enough,*
*much more than I'll ever need. I do it to do it.*
*Other people paint beautifully on canvas*
*or write wonderful poetry. I like making deals,*
*preferably big deals. That's how I get my kicks."*
~ Donald Trump


It's easy to be funny, when you got lots of money,
It fills you with a certain sense of pride.
How easy to be thrilling, with a million dollar billing,
Really sort of cracks you up inside.

Well, you got a ready smile as fortune's footnote child,
And you're loaded to the brim both night and day;
When your debts are paid in full,
Even when you shoot the bull,
People hang on every word you say.
They will haunt you down and find you,
Try to wine and dine you ~ and never let you pay.

So keep a ready smile, when they try to cramp your style,
And the bill collector's knocking down your door,
Say: "I know I'm overdue, but, good morning, how are you?"
Pass on your good will ~ if nothing more.

You'll find you won't have to cheat 'em,
'Cause your attitude will beat 'em.
And even tho a smile won't pay your bills,
Buckle down and win, with a chuckle and a grin;
Magnetize the cash to cure your ills.

You'll find your disposition will insure a new position;
So when people ask the secret of your laughter,
Just say: "Honey, I was funny, even when I had no money,
And that's what changed my before into after!"


© Pat Sampson

99

# The Whistle

When I was a child of seven years old, my friends, on a holiday, filled my pocket with coppers. I went directly to a shop where they sold toys for children; and, being charmed with the sound of a whistle, that I met by the way in the hands of another boy, I voluntarily offered and gave all my money for one. I then came home and went whistling all over the house, much pleased with my whistle, but disturbing all the family. My brothers, and sisters, and cousins, understanding the bargain I had made, told me I had given four times as much for it as it was worth; put me in mind what good things I might have bought with the rest of the money; and laughed at me so much for my folly, that I cried with vexation; and the reflection gave me more chagrin that the whistle gave me pleasure.

This however was afterwards of use to me, the impression continuing on my mind; so that often, when I was tempted to buy some unnecessary thing, I said to myself, Don't give too much for the whistle; and I saved my money.

As I grew up, came into the world, and observed the actions of men, I thought I met with many, very many, who gave too much for his whistle.

When I saw one too ambitious of court favour, sacrificing his time in attendance on levees, his repose, his liberty, his virtue, and perhaps his friends, to attain it, I have said to myself, This man gives too much for his whistle.

When I saw another fond of popularity, constantly employing himself in political bustles, neglecting his own affairs, and ruining them by that neglect, He pays, indeed, said I, too much for his whistle.

If I knew a miser, who gave up every kind of comfortable living, all the pleasures of doing good for others, all the esteem of his fellow-citizens, and the joys of benevolent friendship, for the sake of accumulating wealth, Poor man, said I, you pay too much for your whistle.

When I met with a man of pleasure, sacrificing every laudable improvement of the mind, or of his fortune, to mere corporeal sensations, and ruining his health in their pursuit Mistaken Man, said I, you are providing pain for yourself, instead of pleasure; you gave too much for your whistle.

If I see one fond of appearance, or fine clothes, fine houses, fine furniture, fine equipages, all above his fortune, to which he contracts debts, and ends his career in a prison, Alas! say I, he has paid dear, very dear, for his whistle.

When I see a beautiful, sweet-tempered girl married to an ill-natured brute of a husband, What a pity, say I, that she should pay so much for a whistle!

In short, I conceive that great part of the miseries of mankind are brought upon them by the false estimates they have made of the value of things, and by their giving too much for their whistles . . .

Benjamin Franklin

# DAVID A. COHEN, LLC

Originally from Brooklyn, New York, David moved to Washington D.C. in 1976 to pursue a career in the computer field. He graduated Brooklyn College, CUNY in 1975 with a BA degree majoring in Sociology and Computer Science. He has over 25 years of experience of working with customers in defining requirements, designing solutions and managing the implementation of financial systems and products. Some of the companies he worked for include MCI, EDS, Teledyne Brown Engineering and Commerce One. Today he provides financial planning services for families, individuals, professionals and small businesses by helping them achieve their financial goals with less risk in a tax efficient manner.

David is a family and community oriented person. He has a wife and two daughters and volunteers much of his time within the greater Washington area. He served as President of the Southeast Hebrew Congregation from 1996-1998. During his presidency, he was able to create budget surpluses after nearly 15 consecutive years of running budget deficits and implemented major improvements to the facility. As Banquet Chairman for the Southeast Hebrew Congregation, he successfully ran the highest revenue producing banquets in the history of the synagogue.

- Member of the board of directors for the Yeshiva High School of Greater Washington.
- Member of the Bethesda-Chevy Chase Chamber of Commerce.
- Member of the Greater Silver Spring Chamber of Commerce.
- Member of the Grass Roots Organization for the Well-being of Seniors (GROWS).

**David A. Cohen, LLC, Financial Consultant • AXA Advisors**
**703 205 0390 • 301 681 7155 • dacohen34@aol.com**

# A Financial Check-up

**D**orothy, in the Wizard of Oz said it best when she said, *"there is no place like home."* For us, the support and security of a loving home environment seems even more important today with all the threats of terrorism, layoffs, and corporate scandals. One of the most crucial factors that form the foundation of a positive home environment is the financial health of the family. By taking a few strategic steps with a trusted financial professional, you will shorten the path to your goals and ensure your financial security.

It is essential that you choose a financial professional that you can trust. Working in a consultative relationship allows you to receive professional guidance that supports your lifestyle. With a customized strategy based on your goals and risk profile, you have a better chance of taking the correct course of action. Consider selecting a fee-based plan to obtain an objective financial plan that provides you with general strategies without feeling the pressure to purchase products. As the decision maker ~ you need tools and advisors to give you objective information and advice.

There are three basic steps to follow. First, have your assets diversified into different types of investments. Second, based on your risk profile and timeline, you need the proper asset allocation of those diversified assets. And, thirdly you need to rebalance your assets on a regularly scheduled basis that is based on your proper asset allocation weighting. One of the common mistakes people make is following *what's hot* in terms of performance. They either get in or out of the investment too late ~ and lose a significant percentage of their money. One cannot predict which investment will be the *"right one"* for you. However, working with a trusted advisor empowers you to make informed decisions and take effective actions toward meeting your specific goals.

We all want to take care of our loved ones and ourselves. Whether starting a business, or seeing our children graduate from college or getting married, or retiring early, we all have dreams and hopes. Start today by finding a financial professional that you can trust and get a *"financial check-up"*. Your future in not found "somewhere over the rainbow," or by "tapping your heels three times", but rather right there in your own home.

AGE-26914a  (7/03) (exp 7/05)
Securities and investment advisory services offered through AXA Advisors, LLC (NY, NY 10104) 212-314-4600, member NASD, SIPC

# RENEE OKON

**Renee Okon**, RE/MAX Real Estate Agent, is a graduate of the Realtor® Institute (GRI); and a Seniors Real Estate Specialist (SRES). A woman of great personal warmth, you can't help feeling that you are in the company of a dear friend. When she speaks it is with the sincerity of someone who believes that with hope and determination, anyone can realize the American dream. Born in Nigeria, Renee migrated with her family to the United States in 1969, when she was eleven. After completing school in St. Louis, Missouri, her father encouraged her to pursue a higher education. She received a Bachelors of Science degree in Business Administration from Bradley University. She earned her Masters Degree from the University of the District of Columbia.

Inspired with the entrepreneurial spirit, she opened several successful tax preparation offices. However, the birth of her daughter, Eno-Obong Glory Iquo Okon in 1996, changed her priorities. Loving the home and people, and needing a flexible schedule, she felt it was the right fit to earn a real estate license and later joined RE/MAX, International. It has been a rewarding experience both personally and professionally. Renee is studying for her broker's license and dreams of owning a RE/MAX franchise in the Washington, D.C. area. And one day, Nigeria.

Renee counts her blessings to be in America, but never forgets her homeland. She teaches her daughter to respect and honor them both. Renee firmly believes: "*There are only two lasting bequests we can give our children. One is roots and the other wings.*" Roots let our children know who they are and where they come from. Wings determine how high they fly. But pride of heritage and homeland must be preserved and cherished in order for them to fully derive the benefits of the true American dream."

Contact Renee @ finehomes@ mris.com
(240) 893-2687

# Hope for the Future

*"We should not let our fears hold us back from pursuing our hopes."*

John F. Kennedy

I am often asked about my heritage and my experiences coming to America. I loved my homeland but memories of that time in history are as vivid as if it was yesterday ~ the terror of soldiers storming our village ~ images of my Grandfather and the other men hiding from the threat of capture to fight with Biafrain Rebel Troops. I can still feel the dirt on my hands from digging trenches in which to hide ~ the sound of bombers flying overhead ~ watching as women and children gathered food and necessities for the march to the Federal Troops for protection.

I thank the Heavenly Father for my father, Robert Udo Udo Okon, whose devotion to his family made our new life possible. My father was a visionary who wrote a geography book and sold his copyright to add to the funds from friends and family to pay his way to America. Once here, he earned his pharmacy degree and that became the ticket for all of us to join him in the "promised land".

While we waited for that glorious day, our dear grandmother, and our uncle, the Nigerian Commissioner of Police, kept us safe. I remember the tearful goodbye at the airport and the plane ride with my two brothers to join our parents in Saint Louis, Missouri.

My experiences made it clear to me that there is always hope for the future. We are where we are today – in the present – as a result of what we have experienced in the past. We build on our experiences to find out who we are and what we are made of. We dream our own dreams because of the success and values of those who have gone before us – our parents and grandparents – the founding fathers of this great nation – and the free enterprise system. And then, hopefully, by working hard and keeping hope alive, we can make a difference and contribute to the whole.

You don't have to be a millionaire or a movie star to make a difference. It's about striving to obtain your goals and living to reach your maximum potential. Anyone who cannot succeed in America cannot succeed anywhere else in the world. In this nation, the lowliest beginning is no obstacle to the grandest career. It's also not important that your vision or ambition is as great as someone else's. What is important is to find a profession to which your talents direct you and to make the most of whoever you are.

I believe you can have anything you in this country you want – if you are willing to pay the price. All through my childhood, I heard the message: Make the best of yourself. First you give, and then you receive. Sometimes it takes courage to follow this philosophy. The willingness to give our best, to follow our heart, and to serve others produces success in any endeavor – in our business or personal life. This is the essence of the entrepreneurial spirit ~ the quality that makes one willing to give now in order to receive at some later time. Having done so, we can then greet the future with trust and confidence that we are doing our best in creating a secure future for our families and ourselves.

When I became the mother of my beloved daughter she gave me a whole new sense of purpose and meaning. She is the reason that I get up in the morning. I have a strong desire to provide the best possible surroundings to raise my daughter, and to lead a happy, loving, and productive life. And I wanted to spend as much time as I possibly could to give her the attention our children need and deserve ~ the dilemma of working mothers.

This is when I decided to pursue a career in helping others acquire that big part of the American Dream – home ownership. There is nowhere more special than our homes. It is for most of us a place of comfort and safety, warmth and love. We long for them when away, we dream of having one of our very own, we plan for them, save for them, and celebrate finding them. Real estate agents do a lot more than show houses to prospective buyers. They listen, they observe, they sense hopes and dreams. They know that people are looking for more than a roof over their heads and four walls to protect them from the elements. They help families find a home that comes alive with all the energy of those living within its walls and the interaction that it requires. I wanted to be part of that happening.

I feel so lucky that I have found a rewarding career. I believe that everyone should try to find something special to do with his or her own life. As for myself, it gives me the ability to schedule my time around my daughter's; and the opportunity to earn a good living based on my own merit. I would come to earn all the material rewards that of themselves are nothing, but are great when they represent the courage it takes to make the necessary changes to realize our goals.

I have seen examples of real courage throughout my life. Real courage is a bold adventure in walking forward without looking back. With courage you welcome each new experience as an opportunity to exercise your positive energy in a productive, purposeful direction. You are not afraid of what you do not know; you become eager to learn it. You do not hesitate to extend your efforts into unfamiliar areas because unfamiliar does not mean unfriendly. Real courage is an exercise in facing the truth and allowing it to change your life for the better even when that requires loosening the shackles of habit and responding to old situations in new ways. Real courage doesn't need the security blanket of "this is the way I have always done it". It is free to view change objectively, determine if such change is needed, and, if the answer is yes, implement it without delay.

But unless you know how to give back, your own success will be hollow, because you would have forgotten what the struggle was like . . . and how hard it was to accomplish your goals. You can't always repay those people who helped you directly. But you can do the same thing that others have done for you. That's simply part of the dues you owe to the world. If you've had help, then you're obligated to pass that same kind of strength along to others who may need it.

Before countries can break bread together, neighbors must. The belief in being able to fulfill our own dreams also includes the inspiration of countless people who have already proved that a clear goal and a plan for its achievement inevitably bring success when pursued with determination and confidence. It includes love of family, a clear purpose, and priorities that guide us and keep us moving forward with hope for the future to claim all that life has to offer.

# Hats Off
# to Working Mothers!

"All Mothers Are Working Mothers!"
....Anonymous

It is an awesome spirit that can get up every single day and conquer scheduling, financial planning, and raising children all the while maneuvering through life's curve balls. It is the ultimate management position because working mothers literally manage several lives at a time, while creating healthy, happy human beings along the way.

A mother's love is steadfast through the worst crisis and the loudest cheerleader for the smallest accomplishment. And many do it without the help of a spouse.

You are the warriors because you fight the good fight alone! You set an example of courage your children will never forget! You are very special people and although the path seems twice as hard ~ remember that you are twice as strong and twice as capable or you wouldn't have been chosen for the job! Don't worry about your children's emotional adjustment! Throw away all those articles about the difficulties of lone parenthood and feel confident and proud!

Your children will imitate your attitude, and nowhere is it written that two parents mean twice as much love. Two parents may be preferred, but one loving parent is certainly enough. You may not be able to spend as much time with your children as you like, but it's the quality of those hours that count most. Orphanages are filled with children who have mothers very unlike you.

It's a wonder that you ever have time to cultivate and nurture your own mind, body or spirit. Yet, many of you find time to do that as well, even if it is just a fifteen-minute meditation for strength and courage to carry on. You have raised the bar on what's possible in this world, a contribution that cannot be overlooked. You have a fortitude that enables you to tackle anything that comes your way. And it doesn't come from outside of you ~ it comes from within.

So once again, working mothers everywhere, hats off to you! You are a credit to society, to your children and to yourselves!

# Thoughts on Goals

### Lao-Tzu
The journey of a thousand miles begins with one step.

### Yoda (Empire Strikes Back)
Do, or do not. There is no try.

### Thomas Fuller
He that would have fruit must climb the tree.

### Michael Jordan
If you run into a wall, don't turn around and give up.
Figure out how to climb it, go through it, or work around it.

### Yogi Berra
If you don't know where you are going, you'll end up somewhere else.

### Henry Ford
Whether you think you can, or you think you can't, you're right!

### Donald Trump
I try to learn from the past, but I plan for the future
by focusing exclusively on the present. That's where the fun is.

### Goethe
Whatever you can do or dream you can, begin it.
Boldness has genius, power and magic in it. Begin it now.

### Thomas Edison
I have not failed. I've just found 10,000 ways that won't work.

### B.C.Forbes
How foolish you would be to start on a journey without knowing where
you wanted to go. Have you ever sat down and seriously drawn up a
plan for your life? Have you ever deliberately mapped out where you
want to go during your life's journey? Now, isn't your life infinitely more
important to you than any journey you may take? Why, therefore, not
devote the most earnest effort to plan your life, to set for yourself a goal?

### James Allen
As you think, you travel; and as you love, you attract. You are today
where your thoughts have brought you; you will be tomorrow where
your thoughts take you. You cannot escape the result of your thoughts,
but you can endure and learn, can accept and be glad. You will realize
the vision (not the idle wish), of your heart, be it base or beautiful, or a
mixture of both, for you will always gravitate towards that which you,
secretly, most love. Into your hands will be placed the exact results of
your thoughts; you will receive that which you earn; no more, no less.
Whatever your present environment may be, you will fall, remain or rise
with your thoughts, your vision, your ideal. You will become as small as
your controlling desire; as great as your dominant aspiration.

# JEFF KELLER

**Jeff Keller,** President of Attitude is Everything, Inc., is an attorney who gave up the practice of law to help people realize more from their lives. Author of the best selling book, *Attitude is Everything* ~ the "Attitude is Everything" Newsletter ~ has received high praise from Zig Ziglar and the late Dr. Norman Vincent Peale. For more than 15 years, Jeff has delivered presentations on attitude and motivation to businesses, groups and trade associations throughout the United States and abroad. For more information, go to *http://www.attitudeiseverything.com*

# ATTITUDE IS EVERYTHING!

*"Seek out that particular mental attitude which makes you feel most deeply and vitally alive, along with which comes the inner voice which says, "This is the real me," and when you have found that attitude, follow it."*

~ William James

**Attitude is Everything.** It's the name of my company, and it's a philosophy I endorse with every ounce of my being. I know first-hand how this principle has changed my life for the better. And yet, in my travels, people come up to me and say, "Sure, attitude is important. But is it "everything?" Well ... I truly believe that it is.

Think of your attitude as the "mental filter" through which you experience the world. Some people see the world through a filter of optimism; others through a filter of pessimism. Some see opportunity wherever they go; others see obstacles around every corner. And, of course, most people perceive the world somewhere in-between.

That said, having a positive attitude gives you a significant advantage. First and foremost, people with a positive attitude are optimistic. They focus on "*can*" instead of "*can't.*" They see possibilities instead of limitations.

**Let's examine how your attitude activates the keys to success:**

• **Confidence.** The positive person believes in his or her abilities and strides forward with the expectation of success. Others can see and feel that confidence.

• **Persistence.** We all know the value of making repeated attempts until we reach our objective. Why on earth would you persist if you didn't believe you'd succeed in the long run?

- **Resiliency.** Get back on your feet when you've been knocked down – it's surely one of the most important success principles.

- **Courage.** There's no sustained success without courage. When you believe you can do something, you have the courage to move forward despite being apprehensive.

- **Enthusiasm and Energy.** Show me a person with a dynamic, positive attitude and I'll show you someone who is energetic and, enthused about what he or she is doing. These people have a spring in their step and you feel better just by being around them.

- **Health.** The moment your attitude improves, your health improves. You look and feel younger. The truth is, the cells of your body literally come alive when you're positive.

- **Encouraging Others.** As you begin to use more of your own potential, you're able to see the greatness in others. You have faith in their abilities and they pick up on that! This makes you a far more effective leader.

- **Gratitude.** Positive people appreciate everything more. They dwell on their blessings, and give thanks for all they are given. And this includes the great fortune of being a citizen of a country where they have the freedom to follow their dreams.

- **Perspective.** This is a logical progression of gratitude. You appreciate the many positives in your life and recognize your problems as challenges to be met and overcome.

- **Approachability.** The optimistic person initiates a smile, and you tend to smile back! You feel a certain connection with positive people and enjoy the time you spend with them.

- **Spiritual Growth**. People who commit to developing a positive attitude experience heightened spiritual awareness. You appreciate yourself and others more. You sense you are part of a greater plan – and trust your intuition to guide your life's journey.

Always remember ~ your attitude is a choice that you make every day. The quality of your life ... and the impact you make in the world ... depends on that choice. In the end, I think that you, too, will find that **attitude IS everything!**

# Tricia Walsh, MS

**Tricia Walsh**'s special talent is personal development through physical fitness and training programs that are designed as a tool for building confidence, motivation and self-determination. Her classes are filled with people from all walks of life who all support each other's goals. Her students recognize the importance of having a trainer who genuinely cares about each person's progress and personal success. Her passion for life is positively infectious. She enriches people's lives by giving them new opportunities to fulfill their goals and bring their dreams to life.

Hundreds have taken her training and development programs not only for the joy of physical fitness but for the positive input that is part of every class. "When someone says they can't, I show them how they can", says Tricia. "Helping others to not only look better and become physically fit, but to feel better about themselves is my life's purpose. Once you feel good about yourself and who you are, not only do you become more focused on being the best you can be, but it develops the confidence to handle anything that comes your way".

Tricia's positive outlook on life is a subject she lives and knows a great deal about. As the mother of an exceptional young man with special needs, she has earned the respect and admiration of many for her relentless determination that something higher emerges within us all when we muster the will to face our challenges and grow beyond what we are told is possible.

**Reach Tricia at pscfit@aol.com**

112

# THE POWER WITHIN

*"Two people look out through the same bars;*
*one sees the mud and one the stars."*
Fredrick Langbridge

Life is all about choices. When you are feeling positive, expecting and envisioning the best, you tend to attract the people, situations, and circumstances, which conform to those expectations. Your life is determined not by what happens to you, but how you respond; not by what life brings to you but by the attitude you bring to life.

A positive attitude is an easy concept when everything is going well. It's when life tosses you "curve balls" that you have to dig deep to discover the strength and courage to see you through. I strongly believe that everything in life happens for a reason. As clichéd as that may sound, it is the foundation upon which my life is built. I recognize challenges as part of growth and an opportunity to look more closely at my own attitudes about life and how to respond to it in the most optimistic manner. These are the moments the magic doors swing open. As we free ourselves from limitations, we draw more light and love, not only to ourselves but also to everyone around us.

Just as your body needs physical exercise to maintain peak health and performance so does the mind need nourishment and discipline. Take advantage of every opportunity to discard the negative and don the positive. It's so simple that it sounds almost silly: *change your attitude and you change your life.* But it's a very compelling truth. When you take the time to look on the brighter side it will shine through the darkness ... *every time!*

You have the power to be happy every day. Really! Therefore, the more you are able to imagine and accept your highest good, the more you set it in motion. Be proud of the journey that brought you to where you are. Embrace your inner power with the knowledge that you have something special to offer to the world. Enjoy life and greet each day for the opportunity it truly is. And, most of all, know this: *a strong positive attitude is a rehearsed emotion with your life in attendance!* Make it one to be remembered. *The choice is always yours.*

# Ryan Nicholas Walsh

If any word can be used to describe Cadet Master Sergeant Ryan Walsh, JROTC, Magruder High School Honor Student, it is *"positive"*. The fact that Ryan is in a wheelchair is the last thing you think about when in his presence. His upbeat attitude has always been part of him, and the fact that he has never walked has done nothing to change that. Early on he learned to believe in himself and that he could live up to that potential. "There is never any doubt in my mind that I am loved and that I use the power my mother instilled in me to believe that I can do anything."

Ryan's appearance in *People* magazine would lead to news articles about Ryan and his indomitable spirit, the courage with which he faces innumerable physical challenges, his scholastic achievements, his success as a JROTC cadet, and the national recognition he receives as their number one fundraiser sales star.

Already active with the American Disabilities Association, Ryan envisions a career that merges his interests in law, politics, and psychology as the foundation for his ultimate goal of creating a support system to improve the quality of life for the disabled whether in the workplace, the public arena, or working with government to increase acceptability and opportunity.

Ryan's winning attitude enriches and empowers us all by reminding us that we are motivated by what's inside; and that the ultimate power over our circumstances rests in the minds and hearts of each one of us.

# I AM

I am someone who gets around in a different way,
and loves to dream of what's to come.
I wonder what's in my future?
I hear the voices of my past.
I see my life before my eyes.
I want to be a helpful member of society.
I am someone who gets around in a different way
and loves to dream of what's to come.

I pretend sometimes that I'm a rock star.
I feel I can do anything.
I touch the lives of those who know me.
I worry not about much.
I cry for those less fortunate.
I am someone who gets around in a different way
and loves to dream of what's to come.

I understand that life is what you make it.
I say its not what life hands you
but how you handle life.
I dream of a world of no barriers.
I try to do my best.
I hope that I will make a difference.
I am someone who gets around in a different way
and loves to dream of what's to come.

© Ryan Nicholas Walsh

# ROY PERRY, JR.

**Roy Perry, Jr.** is a winner. A high school student who excels athletically and academically, he represents all young people who develop strong coping skills when family situations change. Roy believes that you have to be self-motivated; that you lead by example; and that you can realize your dreams. But you've got to give it your best. As a little boy, Roy was chosen and photographed with football legend Art Monk, for a magazine cover story espousing positive role models. Roy believes that by realizing his potential he can make a positive impact on the lives of others.

# What I Believe

I believe that whatever happens in your life you can learn from it. You have to hold pictures in your mind of the way you want it to be someday. You have to forget sometimes what you are hearing and even sometimes what you are seeing. Remember – the person who might be criticizing you might have coped out on life a long time ago. As long as you know you are a good person, that's what counts. God loves us all, and all of us are equal in His eyes.

And, we have to take responsibility for that. It's up to us to lay the foundation for a brighter future. Nobody can do it for you. I tell my three younger brothers that they know what's right and what's wrong; if anyone tries to involve them in something they shouldn't be doing, to please confide in me, our parents, or a trusted friend who will help them stay away from negative situations. Getting a good education and finding a positive outlet for your energy, whether that's sports or something else, is a good way to gain the inner confidence to stay on the right track, and to handle things when they don't go your way.

You know, finally, that you compete only with yourself. You realize that it's all about reaching for whatever capabilities you have. You create your own lucky breaks. Nobody can do everything but everyone can do something. Sooner, or later, you find out what your something is. When you are willing to put yourself on the line by taking responsibility for your choices, you can't lose. You are going to win. That's what I believe.

# Prayer for Our Youth

MAY you be powerfully loving and lovingly powerful.

MAY you always have love be your guide with your family, friends, and colleagues.

REMEMBER to listen carefully to your heart and the heart of others.

MAY you have the courage to always follow your dreams.

Take an action every day to support your life dream, your love of nature, and your integrity.

MAY you have the strength to overcome fear and pride, and instead follow what has heart and meaning for you.

MAY you be a guardian of truth, beauty, creativity, and laughter.

MAY you protect, preserve, and care for Mother Nature and the wilderness.

MAY you show respect to people of all ages, and all races, and help all living things keep their dignity.

MAY you help make a better world for the poor, the sick, the elderly, and all the children.

MAY you be an active, committed, and positive force in your community.

MAY you value and maintain your health and the health and well-being of others.

MAY you respect all the ways human beings access their own spirituality.

MAY you create a global community, committed to peace and non-violence.

MAY you keep learning, asking questions, exploring, discovering, and always maintaining curiosity and hope.

MAY you honor and respect diversity and the beauty and magic that occurs when differences join to create something far greater than one could imagine.

MAY you constantly bring your gifts and talents forward every day without hesitation or reservation.

MAY you honor your ancestors and all those who have gone before you, for they have paved the way for you to do what you are here to do.

MAY the butterflies remind you of your soul's beauty and the exquisite contribution that your presence makes in the world every day.

# Best Friends

*A friend is one to whom one may pour*
*Out all the contents of one's heart*
*Chaff and grain together*
*Knowing that the gentlest of hands*
*Will take and sift it.*
*Keep what is worth keeping*
*And with a breath of kindness*
*Blow the rest away.*

~ Arabian Proverb

Your friend knows you for who you are, realizing there are no limits to how great you can become. You share intimate thoughts and feelings because you trust each other unconditionally. You are truly there for each other and can share anything and be whomever it is you feel like being. You are inspired by each other's happiness during the good times and lift each other's spirits during the bad times. Anything he/she can do to help you along the way is a pleasure rather than an obligation. You are patient with each other's faults and weaknesses. You become closer, more open and trusting, and therefore, more supportive during challenging times. You bring out the best in, and want the best for, each other. Your friend believes in you, despite the circumstances and can transfer that belief to you when you need it. Your friend has the kind of faith in you that only comes in true friendship. The kind of friendship ~ that once it comes ~ never goes away.

# SHELTER IN THE RAIN

*"The applause of a single human being is of great consequence."*
- Samuel Johnson

When someone believes in you, it is like shelter in the rain. It sustains you and pulls you through difficult times when endurance is essential. You feel support as you travel life's peaks and valleys. When someone believes in you, encourages you, listens to you and holds a vision of you doing and being your best, that light is absorbed, internalized, and guides you to even greater success.

Recognition for a job well done is high on the list of motivating factors for all of us. When someone is sincerely appreciated for his or her accomplishment ~ whether it be a painted wall, a sales award, a flowering garden, or a completed manuscript ~ that person is inspired to set his or her sights even higher than they have ever dared. Earned praise has a way of bringing out the best in a person. A self-assured person is a messenger of good will wherever he/she goes, as they will be able to navigate life more successfully. Everyone's efforts should be respected and appreciated.

This psychology should be extended not only to family, friends and business associates, but also to the caring cosmetic salesperson at the mall, the considerate clerk at the supermarket and the newspaper boy who delivers your paper dry in a rainstorm. Expressing appreciation makes the world a kinder place. Plus, it has a way of rubbing off on others. Being appreciated for who we are transforms our lives and enhances our awareness in many positive ways.

Our very perceptions of reality are rooted in our early childhood experiences. As we grow, that precious seed must be cultivated so that it grows and blossoms; and we develop the ability to respond to someone outside our own world who might be struggling against all odds. Remember, it is those who are alone and hurting who most need the power of appreciation.

# Julie Jordan Scott

**Julie Jordan Scott** is a writer, speaker and Certified Life Coach from Bakersfield, California. Julie invented "PassionCrafting" a personal development technique incorporating music, visualization, free flow writing, breathing techniques, personal growth and spiritual teachings all in one experience available via recorded CDs or in workshops, retreats and seminars.

The mother of four children, Julie is committed to bringing as many people as possible to experience Passion in everyday life through her website http://www.5passions.com.

# 10 Great Places
# To Meet Passionate People

In my coaching practice and life-in-general I hear one question over and over again: Where can I meet people who share my passionate view of the world?

Since there is no instruction manual for this very real dilemma, I devised this list of possibilities for you to increase your circle of friends, deepen the relationships you have, and give you places to explore to find a wealth of fascinating, intriguing, passionate people. Which will you try today?

Focus for three days upon the one that suits you best. Then, three days later choose another ~ then another ~ and then another. In no time at all, your calendar will be overflowing with dates, your phone will be ringing, and your e-mail box will be flowing beautifully. Here we go ~

*1. Seek out creative arts festivals/events.* Read your local newspaper for listings of such events. Otherwise, ask at places where Creative types gather.

*2. Attend workshops and seminars.* There are countless opportunities to take all sorts of Workshops and Seminars through professional education companies, local religious organizations, bookstores, and college community or outreach departments.

*3. Throw parties with an eclectic blend of people/attend parties with an eclectic blend of people.* As you become a host or hostess with regularity, you will receive return invitations. Be sure to always invite one or two different people from different circles so you can widen everyone's reach.

**4. *Take yoga and other exercise classes.*** Exercising the physical body is a great way to deepen your lessons in personal growth. Befriending the people you meet at classes will inspire you all to continue to grow in each area of the Mind, Body and Spirit.

**5. *Go to poetry readings.*** Great fun for the writers and non-writers among us, poetry readings invite you to explore your own heart in a deeper more profound way. If you are especially brave, sign up to read your work or the work of a poet you admire. Chat with the other poets about their work.

**6. *Participate in political events focused on a proposition or candidate you can wholeheartedly endorse.*** People who spend their time, effort and energy in these areas are usually very passionate as well as outgoing and welcoming.

**7. *Look for spiritual events.*** Perhaps you are interested in exploring another belief system or your own with more depth. A good place to start exploring is in the phone book or in the local newspaper's religion section.

**8. *Do volunteer work for an organization, which is supporting something of special interest to you.*** There are literally groups for everything, be it gardening or grieving or fighting drug use or raising awareness of a particular illness. Simply look around and try one – or two – or three – until you find a match.

**9. *Attend live theatre productions: especially opening events.*** Oftentimes on opening nights, theatre companies will hold special events to celebrate. Strike up a conversation with a couple people you do not know.

**10. *Work in an environment that is in alignment with your calling.*** And if this was reality, imagine the low rate of dissatisfaction in the world! Never stop working towards creating this in your life. It is absolutely possible to find or create the perfect fit. Simply stay alert and focused and follow your intuition.

# KELLY M. BEARD

I have created a balanced life and fulfilling career based completely on "conscious living". And there is nothing more gratifying than watching others do it too. Conscious living means that you're aware and deliberate in the way that you choose to live your life. It's a way of actively integrating your human and Spirit selves, and finding a balanced expression of both. It suggests that there is a Universal energy which is the Source of all life, and yet, it also honors the concept that we have free will and choice to choose how we will express ourselves. Co-creating your life, means that you are willing to work with that energy to strengthen and improve your lifestyle. When you honor both the Universal energy and your human capacity in a balanced way, you can create a happy, healthy and fulfilling life. You can have or do anything you want, if you're willing to work hard, make tough choices and follow your Truth.

Every single one of us is unique, with a unique set of circumstances. My workshop is designed to show you how to: know the tools and choices you have direct access to; know and better understand your unique energy; adapt to inevitable changes; find the lesson or the blessing sooner, rather than later; and ultimately, make better choices on a consistent basis, enabling you to create the life you were born to live!

**Contact Kelly M. Beard**
**Personal Development Coach**
**for more information at:**
*www.Cosmic-Switchboard.com*

# Attracting Your Divine Mate

*"Everything that you are seeking is also seeking you....*
*If you are still, it can find you!"*

Would you marry you? Right now, today? Most people answer with, "not at the moment - maybe in a year or two - I have potential!" That question makes people realize that they have a lot of work to do on themselves, by themselves! You attract all that you are, good and not-so-good. What and who you attract is a total reflection of you. Generally, most of the things you think you are, are based more on other people's opinions, than your own. People judge by appearances and appearances can be misleading. You are the only person who knows the Truth of who you are. The beauty is - the day you begin to truly know your Self, you can begin to redefine your Self!

Everything you need to create a happy, healthy and fulfilling life is already a part of you - you create it all! Not a computer, not another person, no outer entity can create your life! In my workshop, we focus on defining your terms, communication, cycles, unconditional love, and knowing when to let go (and let God). My intention is not to give you the answers, but help you find your own answers. I have set some guidelines and given you various ideas on how to *BE* the person you want to attract.

Paying attention to how you treat your Self is a good place to start looking at how and why you are attracting the type of partners and/ or situations that you are. We go over choices you may not have known (or believed) you had. You always have a choice! You just have to decide what you want and what you're willing to change or give up for what you want. It may be that you don't want to give up anything, so don't! The Universe is limitless and abundant, as are YOU...and you CAN have the dream!

# LAURIE SUE BROCKWAY

**Rev. Laurie Sue Brockway** is an interfaith minister and non-denominational wedding officiant. She is also a spiritual counselor/author devoted to empowering women's self esteem and spirituality. She's a love and relationship columnist for *SoulfulLiving. com*, *LoveMagazine.com*, and *HealthWise Magazine*. She is creator of *Create Your Romantic Resume: A 30-Day Program to Transform Your Romantic Destiny*, available only through *www.selfhealingexpressions. com* and is author of *A Goddess Is A Girl's Best Friend: A Divine Guide To Finding Love, Success and Happiness* (Perigee Books).

# WHEN SOMEONE YOU LOVE PUSHES YOUR BUTTONS...

Nothing is more aggravating in relationships than having your buttons pushed by the one you love. But once the honeymoon period cools and real life sets in, we all take our partners off the pedestal and begin to notice their less than finer points. People often ask me how to fix common relationship problems such as this. Sometimes the best thing to do is just let the dark parts come up so you can shine a light on them.

## Not a Bad Thing

Your partner probably brings up some of the unresolved issues and forces you to revisit and reflect on that within you that needs some attention and healing. Relationships often bring all our "issues" up. Bringing these things to light is not necessarily a "bad thing."

## Lessons to Learn

The people who show up in our lives all have a lesson to bring us or learn with us. When relationships are difficult it is often because they are highlighting a hidden part of the self that we have disowned or weren't even aware of. Intimate relationships beg us to explore our shadow selves. These shadows are not the "boogie man/woman;" they are signs that within lives unknown aspects of self. In many cases, these parts would never be discovered, were it not for the partner who pushes your buttons! The gift is it is a chance to look deeply into ourselves. . . and an opportunity to love ourselves even more by loving "the other."

## Even difficult Relationships are Sacred

If someone shows up in your life to share love, you've been given the great gift of a partner to help you navigate the sometimes smooth, and sometimes choppy, ocean of Relationships. This person can be a romantic partner, a friend, co-worker, or family member. If a relationship or interaction is stimulating or triggering negative emotions or fears, note where this person makes you angry, what about them makes your blood boil; get in touch with ways you feel unloved or upset around them. Then consider they are reflecting something to you that comes from within you. It is one of the hardest lessons for us to learn in life because we always want to point a finger at the other person.

## The Responsibilities of Loving

In these relationships, you may feel that you want to flee… but you cannot flee from yourself. You will only recreate the same pattern elsewhere. When you learn to pay attention to the darker side of relationships and not be fearful simply because it is dark, you will learn which relationships are truly good for you and which you must leave behind. And you will be able to learn which partnerships are ultimately healing and which add injury and insult. This is a process that requires you to take a lot of personal responsibility - to detect and admit your own imbalances and to take on the work of healing them, and by observing and making a decision to alter co-dependent and unhealthy behaviors.

## Steering the Relationship

Love, by its very nature, brings with it a subtle yet sweeping transformative power that brings us closer to our own greatness. But each partner in a love relationship - as well as friends and family members - must get there of their own accord, with love as the gentle impetus, not as the sledge hammer that enforces change. You can't fix your partner, although you can begin to alter your own understanding, behavior and consciousness in the relationship. You can begin to steer the relationship toward a more conscious exploration of the shadowy sides of loving and being intimate with another.

## Know When it's Over

Some people come to us to teach us and then they move on. Some come to learn with us but fail to take away from the relationship the lessons that will empower them to grow. It's important to assess the signs of a partner who has no intention to evolve. The proof here is in the pudding: they simply never make any effort to change and you end up doing all emotional work in the relationship.

You will naturally want to do all you can to help this person along, but there will come a time of reckoning, of absolute truth telling, when you must assess if a relationship has run its course. It is always wise to clarify the differences between getting your buttons pushed as a natural process of relating and being in an unhealthy relationship that is filled with a lot of upset and aggravation.

## Final Word

Talk to your loved one and see if she/he is willing to discuss the situation and find out her/his point of view as well: Is she/he feeling her buttons pushed by you? Telling the truth, and opening the door to telling the truth, is the first step to liberate you and your loved one from a negative pattern you may be stuck in. See if you can open the dialog for some conscious and loving exploration. It's always a more pleasant experience if you and your partner can deal with things in a conscious, loving way. Good luck!

# EVER WONDER?

Where would Barnum be without Bailey?

Where would Roots be without Hailey?

Where would Joseph be without Mary?

The alternatives are scary!

Ever think of Paul Revere

Without his famous horse?

Lancelot without Guinevere

Would have altered history's course.

Some things are part of one another,

It's called a symbiotic freeze.

Usually two ~ depending on each other.

Sometimes ~ they come in threes.

Where would N. B. without C.?

Where would C. B. without S.?

Some things only manage to move

When they meld into a particular groove,

Without each other ~ they're a mess.

What would Nero have done without his fiddle?

Consider Tweede-Dum and Tweedle-Dee,

If you had two ends without the middle ~

What good would the two ends be?

Without some things we would be lost,

They must stick together at any cost.

And if I must further explain ~

Imagine me without you

Or you without me,

And never again complain!

© Pat Sampson

127

# BONNIE PATTERINO

**Bonnie Patterino** has a BS degree from Penn State, is a licensed Esthetician and talented Make Up Artist. Her love of people, art, music and healing therapies inspired her to open a private home Day Spa. She works one-on-one with her clients to enhance individual beauty and personal image. She offers professional skin care, stress therapy treatments, her own custom blend mineral make up, and personal image consulting. Her unique services are described on her Day Spa website: *www.vowsandwows.com*

# Finally Me

I was a gifted child with a natural talent for music, dance and art. I was the youngest of three, always got top grades, and excelled in the performing arts. My family was wealthy, I was pretty, had many friends and appeared to be quite fortunate.

***Instead, I was living in a very dysfunctional family.***

My father was a doctor, but also a manic depressive person who became an alcoholic. Mom tried desperately to keep the peace, but could not subdue his tyrannical behavior. My siblings and I were emotionally and physically abused. Just before college, I started to suffer from anxiety and panic disorder. In 1980, there was no solid diagnosis or effective treatment, so I was left to manage my illness by sheer determination. During that decade, I made new friends and married the love of my life. As I started my professional career, I seemed to be feeling much better.

***I suffered a two year panic and anxiety episode.***

At age 27, I suddenly had a severe anxiety attack which took me into a foggy state, like I was living in a dream, or not in reality. I was functioning at work, but Doctors gave me tranquilizers which made me feel worse. I was secretive about my condition, developed agoraphobia because I was afraid of having an attack in public, and became clinically depressed. With two years of help from a psychologist, I talked out old traumas and began to heal.

Later, it became clear that my condition was due to a combination of a chemical imbalance and childhood trauma. With new medication and therapy, I was able to feel normal again. I can now share my story and empathize with those who suffer from anxiety or depression. It took me years to realize that I was not alone. I have hope, a love for life, and feel like I'm finally me!

# There's No Place Like Home

In a dream, I saw a beautiful woman. She had big brown eyes that sparkled with confidence. Her dark, shiny hair fell softly around her pretty face. I noticed her radiant skin and gleaming smile. She looked familiar to me, but I could not remember why. *"Excuse me, do I know you,"* I asked her quietly. She smiled and said, *"Of course you do."* I paused and asked, *"Who are you?"* She looked me in the eyes and said, *"I'm you!"*

When I woke up, I realized that I needed to make a great change in myself. I had forgotten my own natural beauty. It was easy to see it in others, but not in myself. I knew that if I could start to love and nurture myself, it would inspire others to do the same.

### Forgiveness healed my heart so that I could move on.

My parents have both passed away. They had mellowed as they aged, and in their last few years I understood that they had always meant well. Mom was a submissive personality, but did her best to protect us from harm, and show her love for us. Dad was a good provider, but had suffered from a chemical imbalance and a tough childhood. He self-medicated with alcohol which led to episodes of anger. Understanding this helped me to forgive them and work on bettering myself.

### If I built it they would come...

Several years before mom died, she encouraged me to change my job and work for myself. I had been happier early in my career as an aerobics and fitness instructor. As I worked my way up the corporate ladder, I was financially successful, but increasingly unhappy. It became clear that I needed to find my true calling.

After some soul searching, I took a risk and went to Esthetician school. I trained to be a professional make up artist and skin care therapist. I worked in several Spas for more experience, and then taught at the school while I worked on starting my own business.

I built a private Day Spa in my home, beginning with no clients, no walk-in traffic, and only my vision of an ideal retreat. I wanted my clients to enjoy personal attention, top notch treatments, and a nurturing experience. With very little advertising and lots of referrals, I created more than I had imagined. I now have my own line of custom blend mineral make up, corrective skin care, a unique boutique and loyal clients. Best of all, I invite clients into my home for personal care. They have all supported me and become my circle of friends. I am now the happiest and richest woman I know!

# CINDY B. SINANAN

**Cindy B. Sinanan**, author and real estate agent is an extraordinary woman. She is a homemaker, a mother of three beautiful girls, a children's book author, and a successful member of the business community. As a real estate agent, she quickly established herself as a multi-million dollar producer. Knowledgeable and dedicated, her client lists keep growing along with her reputation as a person with a sense of purpose and commitment. "I treat all of my clients with respect, honesty and fairness to promote as smooth a transaction as possible. I truly care about helping them find the home of their dreams."

Her winning philosophy is based on love for her profession, and a genuine desire to do something creative, beautiful and uplifting for children. Secure in her profession, Cindy expanded on her ambitions and talents to produce a wonderful children's book: *My First Day at School*. The book, inspired by her oldest daughter's experience, covers those moments when children first leave the security of home life and venture into another world. Her daughter, in fact, created the illustrations. The overwhelming positive response has inspired her to continue down that path. "To me the most lasting contribution we can make is to have our children become responsible, giving and trusting adults, but I do not feel that this prohibits achieving personal satisfaction in finding a profession you truly love."

Contact Cindy @ (301)586-9179
email: cindysinanan@mris.com
web: *Cindy21.com*

130

# LOVING WHAT YOU DO

"There is only one success ~
to be able to live your life in your own way."
~ Christopher Morley.

I believe the happiest people are those who have found a profession that they enjoy and have a loving family to support and help them manifest their dreams. These are ideal circumstances but they are within our power to reach.

Once you decide on a career that is best suited to your true interests, first find a positive approach and then focus on your goals. This requires rigorous self-discipline, especially in the beginning. If you are without the financial resources you desire, find a career idea or a service that people need. Your income will rise with your service to others and will provide you with the freedom both to be responsible for yourself and to govern the course of your own life.

Succeeding at your chosen career enriches not only your professional life but also in your personal life. You become instinctively more observant of what is taking place around you ~ in your home, your work, your hobbies, in the marketplace, in the eyes of your friends, and in what your children say. This happens through living the principles of success with courage and faith in your own convictions.

I believe I was destined to enter the real estate profession because of a long cherished love of the family life that is created within and by the home. I feel lucky to work in a field I find so rewarding and hope that everyone can find something equally special to do with his or her own life. When I help people find a special home to surround and enrich their lives, I also help myself become better at my profession. Because family means so much to me – my children are the light of my life - I am happy to be part of helping other families to find just the right place to in which to live and flourish. I hope to be a part of that process for a long time to come.

## The Light of Our Lives

I wish I could put my arms around every child in the world and whisper: *"There is something within you that is only yours, different from everybody else. Every time you learn something new, you discover your own uniqueness, your own special beauty."*

Not all children are as lucky as American children. As free children, they can become all they believe they can be. There are so many wonderful ways to open the windows of their imaginations, so much to see, to learn, to do, so much to read, to touch, to feel, including fairy tales, short stories and carefully selected family movies. The magic of these creative works is that they can awaken young minds to the knowledge that they, too, can reach for the stars. The song "Believe in Yourself" from "The Wiz" sums it all up. And what was "ET" about if not the power of faith, courage, belief? If we give our children enough of this magic – and a lot of encouragement - on a regular basis, they begin to believe in their own abilities.

My husband Chris and I thank the Lord every day for blessing us with three beautiful daughters. They give us strength and energy to accomplish all we can. Our struggles have made us stronger. And today we have so much to offer others. In fact, I authored a wonderful children's book, *My First Day at School*, that was inspired by the emotions of my oldest daughter on her first day at school. It's a story with which every child and parent can identify. My very talented daughter's art enhances it in a heartwarming way.

Thank you for listening. I hope you become a client so I will have the pleasure of listening to you talk about *your* family and children. That's what I love most about my job, having a continuous relationship with all my clients.

Remember me when you are ready to find that dream home where you and your family will create your own memories and live *your own* dreams.

# Thoughts on Home

### Pliny the Elder
Home is where the heart is.

### Helen Rowland
Home is any four walls that enclose the right person.

### Johann Wolfgang von Goethe
He is the happiest, be he king or peasant, who finds peace in his home.

### Christian Morgenstern
Home is not where you live, but where they understand you.

### Henry David Thoreau
What a fool he must be who thinks that his El Dorado
is anywhere but where he lives.

### Ed Howe
The worst feeling in the world is the homesickness
that comes over a man occasionally when he is at home.

### Robert Frost
Home is the place where, when you have to go there,
they have to take you in.

### Algernon Blackwood
A door is doubtless the most significant component of a house.
It is opened and closed; it is where we knock; and it is the
door that is locked. It is the threshold and the limit. When
we pass in through or out of it, we enter a space where
different conditions prevail, a different state of consciousness,
because it leads to different people, a different atmosphere.

### Erma Bombeck
Housework can kill you if done right.

### Anonymous
Thank God for dirty dishes; they have a tale to tell.
While other folk go hungry, we're eating pretty well.
With home and health and happiness, we shouldn't want to fuss;
For by this stack of evidence, God's very good to us.

### Frederick W. Robertson
Home is the place in all this world where hearts are sure of each other.
It is the place of confidence. It is the spot where expressions
of tenderness gush out without any dread of ridicule.

### Chinese Proverb
If there is light in the soul, there will be beauty in the person
If there is beauty in the person, there will be harmony in the house.
If there is harmony in the house, there will be order in the nation,
If there is order in the nation, there will be peace in the world.

# Karen D. Farris

Wisdom teacher **Karen Deborah Farris** is an author, speaker, and workshop leader, and the creator of MESHE, HESHE, MISON & ORBIT -an interactive, unique and practical set of personal development tools. Designed for enlightenment, harmony, enrichment and wellness, MESHE, HESHE, MISON & ORBIT has been taught by Farris in workshops for over two decades. Farris began building a body of writings and teachings in 1983 and incorporates a background in integrated bodywork, counseling and healing. Contact: New Millennium Publishing • (310) 578-5286/6163 • Email: Info@MESHE.com • Website: *www.MESHE.com.*

# The MESHE Concept
## ...A Path to Soulful Living

The MESHE Concept contains a simple practical process for enhancing soulful living. Starting with something as basic as your kitchen, I'd like to show you how you can begin to make soulful choices which will, over time, add up to a more nurturing experience of life.

MESHE (mee-shee) is your "you". Everybody has one. If you are living in MESHE, you are living a soulful life. You are nurtured and centered. You are caring for the little moments, as easily as you care for the grand and important ones.

Many of us try to live our best life by trying to get it perfect. But "perfect" is not something that comes from our center. It is an idea, which comes from the mind. Being in MESHE, is living from the center of your "you." Our center doesn't exist in the mind.

There are many things that keep us out of MESHE. Thinking we need to be perfect is merely one of them.  Worrying is another. My mind repeats a daily list of things that can go wrong, will go wrong, could go wrong, should be wrong. And when I realize I am repeating these worries in my mind, I name that, ORBIT, and the litany stops.

We can move from ORBIT into MESHE as we need to. Being in MESHE means taking all of our moments and being present within them. Not controlling them, or expecting things from them, but rather waking up in the middle and discovering ourselves in what we are doing. The next time you wash your dishes, for example—wake up in the moment—take in the warm running water on your hands, the silky finish of a wet porcelain plate, and be alive inside of the task. That is what it can mean to be in MESHE with something as simple as washing the dishes. Imagine what it could mean to wake up in the middle of dressing your daughter before daycare, greeting your husband when he comes home from a hard day, or sitting on a mountainside after a long well-earned hike.

In my home, I am in an ongoing process of being in MESHE with everything. In my kitchen, I am passionate about my dishes, my glasses, my tableware. I have a cookie jar that makes me smile, a different spatula for flipping eggs than I have for flipping pancakes, and a garlic press that makes clean-up easy. These things are not necessarily expensive. But they are fully appreciated by me each time I use them, because they have expressed some centered part of me from the first day I brought them home. Some things I love because, though money was tight when I bought them, I chose carefully and made sure to buy from my budget something that I liked, something that I was *In MESHE With*. Some things were bought from my heart, putting budget aside. Many treasured items came later than when I first needed or wanted them, because early on, I practiced buying only when I was in MESHE with what I was about to purchase. The same is true for everything that I let into my life—relationships, activities, commitments. It feels better to be in MESHE with not having, than it does to have a lot with which I am not in MESHE.

Maybe it is not your kitchen that needs transforming. Maybe it is your office, your bathroom, or your relationships? Think about it. Being in MESHE in the whole of your life can be a graceful way to wake up and create the necessary changes for which your soul is longing.

Let us go through not just our kitchens, but our entire lives, transforming every task we must do this week, every thought that we think this week, every memory we hash out this week, month or year—until we are in MESHE with all of it!

# JORDAN N. SAMPSON

Jordan's interest in creating magical surroundings led to pursuing a career in the entertainment business as a costume and set design consultant. She offers ambiance planning and insight to anyone who wants to transform private places into special spaces using curios, candles, oils, and genuine stones to create a magical atmosphere reflective of the person's own individuality and sense of fun. Whether gathering your energies to begin your day, or unwinding at the end of one, "Mood Makers" will assist you in creating a world all of your own. E-mail Jordan at *jordansampson@aol.com.*

# Magical Surroundings

Life has a lot of challenges and we have to learn and grow from them. I have discovered that by having a living space that reflects the best of who I am ~ when I step over its threshold my spirit is lifted ~ and I can handle anything that comes my way.

Your space will be different than mine. Find yourself a corner, a room, a city block if that's your style; but pamper yourself with a space that is entirely your domain. Make it a mental health spa where you can relax with a long, cool drink at the fountain of self-appreciation. Let your self-appreciation run wild!

Carpet it in your favorite color, paper it with your favorite feel, and light it according to your mood. Cover a wall with your favorite snapshots ~ even if they're of you! Display gifts from your favorite person (and sometimes that favorite person). Create a treasure box for love letters, funny cards, and theatre programs too sweet to throw away. Keep curios, books, and quotations that feed your senses, soul and spirit. Blare the music, light the candles and soften the mood. Meditate or gyrate. Read, cry, reminisce, or daydream.

It's all up to you!

Having a space dedicated totally to mirroring you, your growth, your humor, your warmth and your attitudes is better than the best medicine available, because it will keep you well and happy. Here you escape to a world designed to reflect and encourage who you are, what you want and where you're going. A world where you feel no pressure only the pure pleasure of letting go! Soak it up! Drink it in! Then go back into the world and give it the gift of your uplifted mood, carrying the joy of you along!

# Create A Collage

"Dwell in possibility!" Emily Dickinson

Let your light shine! Lighten up, fantasize, dream, and play. Imagine what your life would feel and look like if you were living as your most authentic self! Acknowledge your deepest desires about who you are and where you want your life to go. Anything and everything is possible. Let your limitations melt away!

Life is a flow of energy so remove the mental blocks and make way for the good that is coming. Give your imagination free rein to express your creative spirit. Welcome the positive changes that are happening by creating your very own inspirational collage to serve as a guide to new awareness and self- knowledge!

The act of recording images of your deepest desires reinforces your goals. Begin by pasting the most beautiful photograph you have of yourself in the center of a poster, a canvas, or even a wall. Surround it with uplifting quotes from people who inspire you. Write positive words in vivid colors to represent the qualities you most want to attract. Clip pictures from magazines, newspapers, and postcards of your dream house, dream car, and dream vacation. Visualize all the desires for which you long in your heart of hearts. Sketch in your ideal soul-mate ~ that career move you really want to make. Nothing is off limits!

Remember, you can't go wrong. This is your chance to consult with your inner muse. Your energy will soar identifying your deepest yearnings and areas of interest. These self-discoveries will empower you mentally, spiritually, and emotionally to move in an increasingly positive direction to enrich every part of your life.

Believe in yourself, trust that your ideas and goals are achievable, and you will succeed. Once you set your thoughts on paper they enter the concrete world and start to become more of a possibility. It is the first step to achieving your aims. Nourish your spirit by tracking the progress you make with each passing day. Believe! You have the power to make all your dreams come true.

# CHRIS GORENCEL

Chris' desire to become a veterinarian stems from a lifelong devotion to helping others. He is never too busy to lend a helping hand. Throughout his working career, whether as a submarine sailor, computer specialist, carpenter, government contractor, or handicapped therapist, his greatest reward came when he was able to make a positive difference in someone's life. He is a true example of someone who did not compromise his happiness trying to fit in wherever he happened to be. He left a lucrative career at forty to fulfill his life long dream.

Contact Chris Gorencel @ gorencelc@bellsouth.net (or) VZE25f4P@verizon.net.

# Living a Meaningful Life

Living a meaningful life is about more than getting a paycheck. It's about getting up in the morning knowing that somehow you are going to make a difference. Many people wonder what I'm doing in veterinary medical school at my age. Of course, most of the people that ask me are my age or older. My twenty-year-old classmate said she thought it was, "cool." Depending on your perspective, maybe it is.

Veterinary medicine not only gives me the inner satisfaction knowing I am doing something that matters; it stimulates my intellectual curiosity about the animal kingdom. It also provides positive feedback that is so rewarding. If you can find a job that makes you happy every day, don't waste your time in one that doesn't. It took me a while to figure that out; but with the prodding of a dear friend, I took the leap that launched me on my current course. Although I'm working around the clock to learn as much as I can, I find I'm happier these days.

Being a happy person is someone who finds genuine inner fulfillment in his/her activities. You set goals and enjoy the struggles of meeting them, as well as the victory itself. To be happy is to love what you do for a living. You give your best and you give your all. You dream dreams and then channel your energies to make them come true. One day, as a veterinarian, I can apply all of the skills I am acquiring to make a difference in the lives of animals and the lives of their owners as well. That gives my life a profound sense of meaning and purpose. You can't ask for more than that!

# Thoughts on Life

### Henry Van Dyke
Be glad of life, because it gives you the chance to love and
to work and to play and to look up at the stars.

### Joe E. Lewis
You only live once—but if you work it right, once is enough.

### T.S. Eliot
Time you enjoyed wasting is not wasted time.

### Albert Einstein
When a man sits with a pretty girl for an hour, it seems like a minute.
But let him sit on a hot stove for a minute—and it's longer than any hour.
That's relativity.

### Henry Miller
Develop an interest in life as you see it; the people, things, literature,
music—the world is so rich, simply throbbing with rich treasures,
beautiful souls and interesting people. Forget yourself.

### Josh Billings
Life consists not in holding good cards but in playing those you hold well.

### The Upanishads
You are what your deep driving desire is;
As your deep driving desire is, so is your will
As your will is so is your deed;
As your deed is so is your destiny.

### Christian Bovee
When all else is lost the future still remains.

### Scottish Proverb
Be happy while you're living, for you're a long time dead.

### Jack London
I would rather be ashes than dust! I would rather that my spark should
burn out in a brilliant blaze than it should be stifled by dry rot.
I would rather be a superb meteor, every atom of me in
magnificent glow, than a sleepy and permanent planet.
The proper function of man is to live, not to exist. I shall not
waste my days in trying to prolong them. I shall USE my time.

### George Bernard Shaw
Life is no brief candle to me. It is a splendid torch which I have got
a hold of for the moment, and I want to make it burn as brightly
as possible before handing it onto future generations.

# LORI G. DICKERSON

**Lori Gallagher Dickerson** is the author of "Beauty From Ashes," a book born of her own experience with clinical depression. While in the throes of this illness ~ writing helped her cope with the intense pain and confusion that are a part of this disease. It is an attempt to offer comfort and encouragement to those experiencing depression.

Lori, a Registered Nurse, lives in Tupelo, MS., with her husband and three children. Her book is available online at publishamerica.com, Amazon. com, Barnesandnoble.com or your local bookstore. Contact Lori at phil4-13@netdoor.com.

# Can A Caterpillar Fly?
## RELEASE FROM CLINICAL DEPRESSION

You bet it can! But it will not happen without transformation, a change that requires both time and introspection. That small caterpillar represents great potential. When nature is allowed to take its course, she becomes one of the most beautiful creatures on earth.

I have felt very much like that lowly green caterpillar. Clinical Depression has plagued my life for the past three years. It seems that when you are in the caterpillar stage of this illness, it is very difficult to visualize the butterfly that is inside just waiting to emerge. At times, the hopelessness and despair have become so great that it was much easier to imagine a world without me at all.

Have you ever watched a caterpillar crawl across the sidewalk? It is truly slow going, but she trudges ahead and keeps pushing forward until she reaches the safety of the grass on the other side. Along the way she encounters rocks, the threat of big feet, and other insects hungry for a meal.

This accurately describes how it felt to be admitted to Behavioral Health at the local hospital. The rocks became the locked door that surrounded me. The big feet became my own negativity that threatened to crush my very being. The hungry insects became some of the hospital staff whose only purpose it seemed was to humiliate their patients. But I trudged on. The medication prescribed for me seemed to ease the depth of my emotion.

Before the caterpillar can become a butterfly she must cocoon. The hospitalization proved to be very traumatic for me in spite of the lessons gained. I came home feeling shameful, and guilt-ridden. Shameful for the weakness that I believed caused me to have to go to the hospital in the first place, guilt-ridden for having the unacceptable thoughts of giving up on life. I was terrified at the thought of having to face anyone outside my home. The shame caused me to turn inward. Just as the caterpillar spins her cocoon around her, a protective shell that envelops her - I pulled inward. I created a sort of cocoon within my own bedroom. It was there that I began to journal my thoughts and feelings. Sitting in my overstuffed chair I could re-live the therapy sessions that had become as necessary as breathing, meditating on the words that were said during the short time spent with my counselor, giving them a chance to take root within my thoughts.

I rediscovered my faith in God and the power of prayer. It took great courage to allow myself to be admitted to a mental hospital. I needed help and in spite of the stigma attached to such a place, I went where I knew that help was available. I am actually a very strong person - a weak one could not have endured the trials I have faced as a result of this illness.

Do you wonder what it feels like to emerge from that dark, lonely, cocoon? I know. It is a bit scary, actually. But the world seems incredibly bright and full of promise. The butterfly has a choice. She can simply stay on her branch all safe and secure, or she can spread those magnificent wings and fly away, meeting her greatest potential.

During my time spent in introspection I changed. Just as the caterpillar stage will always be a part of the butterfly's life, the time I spent battling my depression will be a part of mine. But the butterfly does not allow that necessary stage of her past to hold her back, and neither will I. The going is shaky at times, but I will continue to soar.

There is a very special job awaiting the newly emerged butterfly, that of pollinating the flowers around her. I truly understand what it feels like to go through a depression. I know the pain of hopelessness and despair so great that it is overwhelming. I feel the joy of becoming myself again. Now I can share that with those who follow me. I can offer hope because I have been there and have come out on the other side. That doesn't mean it is smooth flying. But now I rejoice when trials come my way. I see them as an opportunity to make myself even stronger and to make the colors of my wings even more vivid.

Now would someone please open the window? I have some flying to do!

# KEEP THE FAITH

*"If all misfortunes were laid in one common heap whence everyone must take an equal portion, most people will be contented to take their own and depart."*
~ Socrates

It is easy to be courageous when life is treating you well. But when you are met with experiences that test your faith, when plans go astray and hurts sadden ~ hope wanes. When circumstances threaten your very survival ~ requiring a supreme concentration of energy and superhuman strength to endure without weakening over a long period of time ~ your dreams may be drained of the faith that, if followed, would have made them come true. It is a time of no guarantees, a time of uncertainty, and perhaps even chaos.

Just as a construction site is a jumble of bricks and boards before the new building rises through the disarray, so does life sometimes appear hopelessly confused. Every principle you have ever studied and every experience you have ever had is called upon to stretch your mind, your emotions, and your faith to heights you were unaware were within your reach. It is true that if you keep fear from moving in, you find resources at your command that you never dreamed possible.

You become a master at generating self-inspiration to nurture and sustain your spirit. Your courage under pressure will show you how to fall without getting hurt, and how to get up over and over again. You will become stronger than you ever imagined. Focusing on thepositive changes you want to make empowers you spiritually and emotionally and strengthens your resilience. Your inner being ~ the core of your strength ~ whispers: *"Hold on. You'll make it. There is work to be done."*

If there were no magic in the power of believing, we would soon stop believing. But we don't. We go on in the face of incredible obstacles and overwhelming odds that transform circumstances beyond physical explanation. Even if your world crumbles, you have the power to put it back together and with renewed confidence create the best outcome you can imagine!

# SCARS TO STARS

*"I don't think of myself as a poor deprived ghetto girl who made good. I think of myself as somebody who from an early age knew I was responsible for myself, and I had to make good."*
~ Oprah Winfrey, Super Star

Along life's voyage, you may become wind-burned, weather-beaten, and battle-scarred. Your scars can be your victories if they represent obstacles overcome, detours averted and limitations defeated. Every one meets with wounds along the way; some are no more than annoyances, while others may be nearly fatal. Some can be anticipated, while others come as complete surprises, but there are no wounds that cannot be healed, no matter how deep, or how permanent they seem.

A worthy traveler never uses wounds as an excuse to quit. The little scratches you ignore; the big ones you bind as best as you can. You persevere not only for yourself but for others who look to you for guidance and inspiration. Realize how often fate offers surprise packages disguised as bad breaks awaiting only your initiative to remove the wrappings and view the treasures within.

There are those whom the mightiest upheavals leave unscathed, those who seem to be anchored securely to a center of peace and well-being. Their attitude is uplifting, their presence reassuring; their confidence awe-inspiring. They have made a commitment to the mastery of their souls.

They have pledged allegiance to all that is positive and life-giving. They have united themselves with the most powerful forces in the universe ~ goodness and truth. They have turned their backs on defeat, closed their minds to negativisms, and refused to entertain any alternatives except those leading to success.

They are life's super stars, the honored among their peers: those who have assumed the responsibility and initiative for the quality and course of their lives, whose lives serve as a shining reminder that nothing believed possible is impossible, and that all things are possible to those who believe.

# JENNIFER L. JOHNSON

I can still see his eyes as he was the first time we met. The cold July rain clung to my face and hair, the music blared from the side stage, and we sat in the mud (whose idea was it to call them "lawn" seats?) at Lilith Fair. He was lying back on his blanket in front of my friend and me, and when he looked up with his sparkling steel blue eyes and roguish grin, I should've known that my life would never be the same.

Months later when he left me (without a word) I fell apart. I was broken, scarred, and scared. I was terrified of loving like that again, but worse, of not trusting people and walling myself in. I reached out for anything – anyone – who could comfort me and help me understand. I found Reiki.

My Reiki Master guided me as I began pursuing the healing arts. While finishing my undergraduate degree I furiously delved into my spiritual and healing studies – if I couldn't understand what had happened, then I was determined at least to understand myself! Despite my evening and weekend professional training classes (in Reiki, Hypnotherapy, etc.) and my 21-credit undergraduate course load, I was happier than ever before:

At age 21, I had found my purpose.

**Jennifer L. Johnson**, RUDP, CRM, LBLT
**Executive Director/Founder**
**Center for Inner Power, Inc.**
*www.CenterForInnerPower.com*
**call the center at 540-548-c4ip (2447)**
email *info@centerforinnerpower.com.*

# LIVING YOUR PURPOSE

**Why am I here? What's the point of it all anyway? Can I really make a difference? How?!?**

Questions of purpose can be some of the most difficult ones we ask throughout the course of our lifetime. They do not have easy answers and usually take quite some time to understand. And even when we figure them out, the answers continue to change and evolve as we do. So why do we even ask? Because… we're human.

I believe we each have three types of purpose: personal growth/ evolution (a goal common to us all), our "mission" or life's work, and our soul's spiritual purpose. While they can be addressed separately, I like to view them as a whole under the general label of purpose; the triad being more powerful united than separate.

Purpose is essentially a contract we've chosen to come here and fulfill based on our skills, weaknesses, and past experiences. It's different than the Western idea of fate (something imposed upon us by external forces), in that, from this perspective, even painful situations have great meaning and are not viewed as punishment for some earlier wrong. Choice grants us more responsibility than a simple law of karmic cause and effect, as the purpose of all things becomes understanding and forward growth. We choose how we respond to circumstances presented to us; for events we cannot change, we choose how to react.

But all of this information does you no good if you don't already know your purpose, right? I mean, maybe you'll able to recognize it when it comes along, but what if you don't?

Finding purpose is one of my greatest passions since I've felt the effects it has had in my own life. When I started working with this professionally, I was surprised to realize just how many people lack understanding of their own purpose, wisdom, intuition, and inner power (hence the name of my center). One of the most surprising things I found though, was that even those who were *exactly where they needed to be* wanted reassurance that they truly were on the right path.

As my skills grew and my studies deepened, I found that helping others find their purpose comes naturally to me. I use many techniques for this, but my favorite is Life Between Lives Spiritual Regression (as taught by Michael Newton, PhD, author of *Journey of Souls* and *Destiny of Souls*). In this method, we use hypnosis to contact your higher soul self so that you can find the answers that already exist within you. In conjunction with this, I always advise getting more actively involved in your life. Do those things that you've always wanted to do. Take that poetry class or start experimenting with clay. Volunteer as a big brother or big sister if you've always wanted to work with kids, or join the community choir if you long to sing. *Do Something.* If you at least do that, I guarantee you'll eventually stumble across your purpose.

*"Purpose is essentially a contract we've chosen to come here and fulfill."*

Most of us know when we're doing something that's wrong for us – we feel guilty or get a queasy feeling in the pit of our stomach – but we also tend to know when we're doing something purposeful (even if we disregard it). When our actions support our life's purpose we feel a sense of accomplishment and even duty. We are challenged in ways we could never have dreamed of, and those challenges keep us going longer than we thought we were able.

When we're walking along our path, fulfilling the seemingly inconsequential trials and nuances of our purpose, everything else begins to arrange itself. That perfect job opportunity materializes out of the blue; a person appears to explain (or illustrate) that concept we'd been grappling with; events line up so we can show both ourselves and others what we're truly made of. The flow of our lives becomes effortless, while the obstacles force us to find new and creative ways to overcome them. It's both easier and more difficult at the same time.

Living your purpose means you're "on-call" twenty-four hours a day, three hundred and sixty-five days of the year. Every person you meet is in your life for a reason, and you begin to notice those reasons. "Good/bad" and "right/wrong" lose their power, as you come to understand that everything just "is." You may even find (as I did) that what you originally perceived to be the worst possible heartache, disappointment, or event to happen to you was one of the absolute best possible situations because of how you grew from it. Imagine being able to look at those heartaches and painful trials as blessings.... *Can you picture yourself filled with love and gratitude for the people who hurt you the most?*

When you live in a way that is true to your own purpose, there · is no need for regret, guilt, or blame. Everything you've done, every person you've met, and everything that's happened to you occurred just as it was supposed to.

The bottom line is always the same: trust your inner wisdom and power. And if you're ever unsure, just remember that by virtue of asking, you are exactly where you're supposed to be at this moment in time.

And *that's* a comforting thought.

---

Services offered at Center for Inner Power, Inc. include:

Life Between Lives Spiritual Regression, **Ultra Depth**® Hypnotherapy, Deep Memory Process, Kinesis™ (a.k.a. Telepathic Communication Technique™), Soul Readings/Spiritual Counsel, Young Living™ Essential Oils and treatments (Vita Flex and Raindrop techniques), Spiritual Healing (including Traditional Usui Reiki, guided imagery/visualization/meditation and breathwork, chakra balancing, gem/crystal healing, psychic protection, etc.), Massage Therapy, Reiki Certification, Training Classes, and a metaphysical store!

# KATHERINE RABENAU

**Katherine Rabenau** (also known as Ravenlea) finds her bliss as a writer, a Reiki Master Practitioner and through using sound as a healing tool. Her e-book *How Do I Get Out of Here? An Insider's View of Agoraphobia* is available through The Writer's Closet - *http://www.writerscloset.com*. An explanation of Reiki is available on her Raven's Reiki website – *http://www.geocities.com/ravensreiki*. Information on her *Love Tones* CD is available at *http://www.geocities.com/krabenau/lovetones.html*. Or you may contact her at *Krabenau@aol.com* with inquiries on any of the above.

# Finding Our Bliss

As I get older, and hopefully a bit wiser, I have come to believe that one powerful chord underlying the music of bliss is gratitude. Not long ago someone sent me an article by a man named Alan Cohen in which he shared a powerful mantra that goes as follows: *"Thank You for Everything. I have no complaints whatsoever."* I decided to try it. The more miserable the crisis I seemed to be facing, the more enthusiastically I chanted my gratitude, and much to my amazement not only did my feelings about whatever individual drama I was dealing with at the moment change, my life began to change as well. Gratitude is an expression of love. It is an expression of joy. Gratitude puts our attention on what is good and reinforces it. Gratitude helps us to embrace our blessings. Hawaiian mystics have a saying that goes "energy flows where attention goes;" they teach the concept that whatever we bless (pay attention to) in this life we bring to us. (If you spend a day or a week – or even a few hours – looking for things to bless, you'll be amazed at how uplifting it can be. It's hard not to feel better about life when you are looking for and focusing on the many wonders that surround you.)

So why is the *"thank you for everything"* mantra so powerful? Gratitude is an expression of love and love is the most powerful force in the Universe. Love changes and enriches everything that it touches so when we bless – give thanks – for all our experiences we alter them for the better. Acknowledging the hand of the Divine in every moment and event enables the Universe to lavish even more love and blessings on us. Blessing all our experiences puts us in harmony with the Divine Plan. *"Thank You for Everything. I have no complaints whatsoever,"* is an expression of Love and the most sacred form of Trust. It connects and aligns us with our truest Self because when we say it, we are owning our relationship to All That Is and we become a living, breathing expression of Love. We become who we truly are. And that is bliss indeed.

# Thoughts on Happiness

### Robert Browning
Make us happy and you make us good.

### Don Marquis
It is better to be happy for a moment and be burned up with beauty
than to live for a long time and be bored all the while.

### Art Linkletter
Things turn out best for the people who make the best
out of the way things turn out.

### Norman Lear
Life is made up of small pleasures. Happiness is made up of those tiny
successes. The big ones come too infrequently. If you don't have all of
those zillions of tiny successes, the big ones don't mean anything.

### Patanjali
When you are inspired by some great purpose, some extraordinary
project, all your thoughts break their bonds; your mind transcends
limitations, your consciousness expands in every direction, and you find
yourself in a new, great and wonderful world. Dormant forces,
faculties, talents become alive, and you discover yourself to be a
greater person by far than you ever dreamed yourself to be.

### Hannah Senesh
One needs something to believe in, something for which one can have
whole-hearted enthusiasm. One needs to feel that one's
life has meaning, that one is needed in this world.

### Beran Wolfe
If you observe a really happy man, you will find him building a boat,
writing a symphony, educating his son, growing double dahlias,
or looking for dinosaur eggs in the Gobi desert. He will not
be searching for happiness as if it were a collar button that
had rolled under the radiator, striving for it as the goal itself.
He will have become aware that he is happy in the course of
living live twenty-four crowded hours of each day.

### Ralph Waldo Trine
No clear-thinking or clear-seeing man or woman can be an apostle of
despair. He alone fails who gives up and lies down. To get up each
morning with the resolve to be happy; to take anew this attitude
of mind whenever the dark or doleful thought presents itself, or
whenever the bogeyman stalks into our room or across our path,
is to set our own conditions to the events of each day. To do this
is to condition circumstances instead of being conditioned by them.

# John de la Vega

**John de la Vega** was born in Buenos Aires, Argentina, came to America to fulfill a childhood dream. At fifteen he launched a distinguished career in portrait painting of ever increasing success. He has painted many famous personalities: President Ronald Reagan, show business and sports figures, and CEO's from the nation's top corporations. Other pursuits have included undergraduate and graduate studies in Psychology at The American University, Washington, D.C., composing contemporary classical music for the piano, creating and conducting the Thou Art Seminar in Art and Successful Living, and teaching workshops on painting. John de la Vega can be reached at johndelavega@aol.com

## The Importance of Art

Art today is both more present and more absent from our lives than ever. In its most creative forms, it has filtered down to affect many aspects of our daily existence, as, for example, advertising, a creative activity using many of the "higher" principles of art and beauty. We are also exposed to and influenced by art as design in its many forms, in artifacts that we enjoy in our daily living.

This does not mean that our awareness of art as a spiritual force is as rich as we might desire for our development as humans. Perhaps today we need exposure to art in its "purer" forms more than ever, besides to its products for living and entertainment. I believe it urgent for societies to really get to know the best we have produced in art in order to attain an ever higher spiritual and intellectual growth. If individually and collectively we become more aware of deeper artistic principles and beauty, our lives can in themselves become deeper, more creative, joyful, certainly more positive.

The higher, more meaningful products of art are everywhere around us. We no longer have to live in a big city to see great works in museums or to enjoy theatre, music, ballet, opera, besides art through the written word. Books, magazines, television and the Internet offer full servings of the best of art past and present, ready for us to seek out, enjoy, and grow from. Yes, it does take a certain attitude, intention, interest and even effort to eschew the fast food of easy entertainment and go for the real goods, the deeper beauty. But the rewards are immense, not only to our lives, but also to the lives of all the coming generations.

Art, like love, is in everybody's soul. It is as close as going within in silent meditation to without to contemplate the exquisite design and grandeur of nature, all of it the work of the supreme artist, His gifts of great beauty and harmony ready for us to claim.

# Thoughts on Art

**George Santayana**
An artist is a dreamer consenting to dream of the actual world.

**Sir Joshua Reynolds**
A room hung with pictures is a room hung with thoughts.

**Heywood Braun**
The artist has never been a dictator, since he understands better
than anybody else the variations in human personality.

**Johann Wolfgang von Goethe**
A man should hear a little music, read a little poetry, and see a fine
picture every day of his life, in order that worldly cares may not obliterate
the sense of the beautiful which God has implanted in the human soul.

**Oscar Wilde**
No great artist ever sees things as they really are.
If he did he would cease to be an artist.

**Maxwell Anderson**
If you practice an art, be proud of it and make it proud of you.
It may break your heart, but it will fill your heart before it breaks it;
it will make you a person in your own right.

**Mark Twain**
Can it be possible that the painters make John the Baptist
a Spaniard in Madrid and an Irishman in Dublin?

**Bernard Berenson**
I wonder whether art has a higher function than to make me feel,
appreciate, and enjoy natural objects for their art value. So, as I
walk in the garden, I look at the flowers and shrubs and trees
and discover in them an exquisiteness of contour, a vitality of
edge or vigor of spring as well as an infinite variety of color
that no artifact I have seen in the last sixty years can rival.

**Leo Tolstoy**
Art is a human activity consisting in this, that one man consciously,
by means of certain external signs, hands on to others feelings
he has lived through, and that other people are infected by
these feelings, and also experience them.

**Ordway Tead**
Make the work experience you select as fully as possible your own
channel of distinctive creative effort, where you are at once,
making a contribution derived from your talents, and by so doing, are
enriching the productive life of society – in business, art, education,
social work, at home, or in some other of a thousand outlets.

# DOUG HYDE

**Doug Hyde**, designer for this book, has donned many hats in his lifetime. The son of a prominent surgeon, he always preferred to "march to the beat of a different drummer." He earned a degree in government and politics paying for it by working full-time as a miner on the Washington subway system. After graduation, he attended welding school and worked as a miner-welder, mechanic, pile-driver, and a fabricator for the next twelve years. Drawn to academia, he attended community college and while enrolled in a drafting course he discovered the graphic design field. At age 38, throwing caution to the wind, he quit his high-paying construction job to take entry-level work as a designer. In 1991, growing tired of the constraints of the corporate world, he embarked on a freelance career and founded HyTech Design.

My approach to life has always been to strive to obtain perfection. As an artist my goal is to try to render true and absolute beauty, knowing full well that I will never do so. However, it is that pursuit of perfection that guides my life in all of its facets.

I've always taken great pride in my work, trying to do it the best way possible. "Doing my own thing" has cost me various jobs, but being true to my vision has always given me great satisfaction. Switching from high-paying positions to work that is more emotionally and creatively fulfilling (though much lower paying), has taught me the value of self-reliance and helped me remain true to myself.

My search for beauty in the world has driven my life in so many ways. With my knowledge, skills, and passion, I can make my "electronic" canvas come alive. It is a thrill and a challenge to pull together disparate elements to create a visually-stimulating design that communicates and motivates the audience. I always aim to give the client more than he expects. In my personal life, I find creative fulfillment in painting and photography.

Immersing myself in the art world has allowed me to appreciate the aesthestic side of people and life. My intense desire to create beauty is what drives me and keeps me alive.

**Contact Doug at (703) 256-1150 or
dhyde@hytech.com.
Visit his website at *www.hytech.com***

**Sean Hill** currently does free-lance work for a variety of businesses large and small. A self taught illustrator, musician and computer artist he has worked for various visual communication companies, primarily producing marketing and promotional designs. Having been an award-winning graphic designer and illustrator for over fifteen years, he has been privileged to create alongside some very inspired and talented colleagues. In 2002, he achieved an APEX award for a series of marketing designs for EPI Communications, giving the company another consecutive award-winning year.

One of humankind's earliest efforts at communication was through drawing. Today, communication is made in many different ways and forms, whether it reaches us by talking, hearing, writing, singing or even dancing. Visual communication in magazines, newspapers, billboards, television... everywhere, plays a large part of everyone's life.

Design is the considered arrangement of images that produce a desired result or effect. Harmony, balance, rhythm, movement, unity and contrast are all part of the symmetry of designing. Much like a symphony, its form consists of several themes, which repeat and change throughout its composition. This pattern stands true in the approach of all design. It is the art of the graphic designer to create symmetrical or asymmetrical patterns, with contrasting shapes and rhythmic lines in order to present the viewer with a feeling of both unity and balance.

I have always felt that the basic elements of design parallel the elements of healthy living. Everyday life is a sure inspiration to me when it comes to creating a theme. Whether the vehicle is humorous, serious, political or current affairs, it is a deeply satisfying feeling when something I illustrate catches the publics' eye. Inspiration is truly my creative impulse. I believe "Eye Candy" is the best way to describe my approach to design. I like a powerful strong impact to catch the eye of the viewer and to hold the interest. Nothing is more rewarding than knowing that I can be a part of someone's business growth through the help of visual communication.

**Contact Sean: (301) 482-1208**
**seanhill2000@aol.com**

# Deborah Eby

**Deborah Eby** has served as a writing and editing consultant to many holistic, business, nonprofit and news organizations for more than 20 years. Her broad experience spans the field of print media, including authoring two books on holistic health and conscious living as well as writing and editing numerous articles, websites, reports, marketing literature, and media packages. She also teaches professionals how to produce creative, effective business writing. Deborah helps her clients communicate with soul, spirit, and expertise.

Words are the way we communicate our beliefs, ideas, and information. Words carry the energy and power of their writer's purpose. From ancient holy texts to Shakespeare to the U.S. Constitution, compelling documents guide and inspire humanity for centuries and millennia beyond their writers' lifetimes.

The communications revolution has opened for us an unprecedented opportunity to access knowledge and wisdom from around the globe. We also have the chance to spread our own creative ideas and solutions to all those who would benefit. Clear communication through effective language has never been more important.

Mass media have made us aware of our global interconnection. We understand more clearly every day that the talents and strengths of each one of us are necessary for a thriving, healthy planet. Attorney, artist, healer, merchant, entrepreneur… whatever your forte, someone who needs your help is waiting to connect with you. All successful business, after all, is founded on service to others.

Options abound for telling other people how you can serve them. Whether you reach out with a website, book, brochure, ad or article, craft your words carefully. Your written message may be your first and last chance to capture the attention of someone who needs what you can offer.

**Clarity Ink—Making Your Message Crystal Clear**
**Deborah Eby—Writing, Editing, Effective Writing Seminars**
(703) 759-4787  *deboraheby@aol.com*

# BLUE NILE BOOKSTORE

## ILLUMINATIONS FOR ENLIGHTENMENT

Blue Nile Bookstore is a labor of love and a ray of light ~ a one of a kind gift shop ~ sharing positive energy through an assortment of books, crystals, music and jewelry.

Our books are carefully selected to serve as guides and teachers for those seeking truth in all phases of life, and we have compiled a unique array of tools to assist you in remembering the importance of Spirit.

The spiritual path is not always easy. Those of us who have decided to seek the light often need to be reminded - and sometimes coached - so as not to forget our responsibility to carry the ray of light within us and in so doing attract and assist others.

One of our main attractions at Blue Nile is the Aura Video Station, a unique bridge between technology and spirituality. Using the latest bio-feedback technology and digital imagery to discern the light around the body (the aura), this computer also displays the color, shape and size of the body's charkas. This is a powerful tool for getting at the heart of personal conditions that may need attention. We also offer computerized astrology charts that reveal natal, progressed and compatibility astrology information for those curious about their life's purpose and mission. There are classes available in astrology, numerology, reiki, massage therapy and other healing arts.

We are extremely proud of our crystals, particularly the lemurian crystals from Brazil and turquoise and lapis jewelry from New Mexico. Crystal lotus flowers and chakra colored glass candle burners are among the unique gift ideas intended to remind us to acknowledge Spirit. To support those who mediate, heal and contemplate, we offer selections from the latest new age music vendors.

Blue Nile Books is at the forefront of this new and exciting age of light. We are honored to be an extension of love and light and service to humankind. We welcome you to come in and experience the wonderful store we have created for you.

**BLUE NILE BOOKSTORE**
2828 Georgia Avenue, N.W. Washington, D. C.
202-232-2583 Monday Saturday Noon to 7 p.m. Sunday- Noon-4 p.m.

# SANDY YOUNG

## SPIRITUAL TEACHER & HEALER

Sandy Young, Co-Guardian, TeleSpectral, Living Light Center, has been featured on public television, national and local radio programs, and is presently completing her book of angelic readings. Sandy has worked on research projects with Dr. Norman Shealy and is an ordained minister, spiritual teacher, healer and alternative health practitioner. Sandy's ability to understand the human heart, to feel the turmoil that others like herself experience day to day, and knowing the reason why things happen, began when as a young child she telepathically communicated with her grandmother. It came so naturally that she thought everyone could do it. Her gifts grew and transcends the usual boundaries of communication, hearing and seeing the angelics and passed over loved ones, talking with pets and nature, reading the Akashic Records with the clarity of reading a book are all in line with the oneness of all things that Sandy holds as an ideal. She has a deep desire to give to others, to share, and to contribute to the greater good of all. She truly cares about the happiness and well-being of others.

Sandy and her husband, Jim Young, established The Living Light Center to offer many healing modalities that strive to bring balance to the body, mind and soul in oneness. Services offered include: *Angelic Readings, Sound Therapy, Oxygen Ozone Steam Sauna, Voice Analysis, Ear Candling, Reiki & Seichim.* Visit the Living Light Center soon. It's an experience that will stay with you for a lifetime.

**Arrange for a personal reading by phone ~ or in person:**
**(301) 990-4966**
*www.LivingLightCenter.org*

# THE LIVING LIGHT CENTER

*"Outside the open window,*
*The morning air is all awash with angels."*
**~ Richard Wilbur**

The Living Light Center is a place where people come to enjoy the energies of the Crystals in an all glass Sacred Room. Surrounded by an Oriental Japanese Fish Pond, four winding stone pathways, connected to an 8-foot and 4 foot stone spiral at each end with an 8-foot x 8-foot stone pyramid one may sit in for meditation. Sitting quietly, you can feel the energy vortex radiate around the property so beautifully that it seems to pull the surrounding trees from other properties toward it. A sacred space where bumblebees and squirrels come when you call them. It is a place where doves and chipmunks share the same food source together in harmony. The Living Light Center is where crossing the threshold of tomorrow is today. And, of course, during your visit, you will have the opportunity to meet two very spiritual lights in our world, Sandy & Jim Young, Co-Guardians of the Living Light Center.

Recently, Jim Young shared this insight into the meaning the Angelics have brought into his life.

> "There was a time before meeting Sandy that the thought of an Angel being personally involved in our lives was beyond my experience. Very soon after, I began to see and experience their presence, and realized they were always near, and willing to offer assistance in any way they could if only asked to do so. The last few years have brought so many twist and turns in the path and such profound changes that had we not had the wonderful gift that Sandy has been given, I cannot imagine what the outcome would have been. The ability to know the reasons why things happen or how the choices along the path may play out, were invaluable. Know that they are here for you too."

---

## A GIFT OF LOVE & LIGHT

The reader of this book may ask one question of the Angelics on any subject, through a reading by Sandy at no charge through the Information Form @ www.LivingLightCenter.org. Please know this is for a limited time.

# VALERIE RICKEL

**Valerie Rickel** is the founder and creator of SoulfulLiving.com, a highly publicized internet community and monthly web magazine dedicated to personal and spiritual growth. Born into a family of artists, Valerie was educated at UCLA and combines her background in psychology, her keen eye for exquisite design and detail, and nearly a decade of marketing and public relations experience into all her ventures. A web developer, marketing consultant and author, she is known by the business moniker, *The Creative Soul* ®. Valerie is currently at work on a series of *Soulful Living* ® books. E-mail Valerie at valerie@soulfulliving.com, website: SoulfulLiving.com.

*SoulfulLiving.com* is an award-winning monthly web magazine and popular internet community dedicated to personal growth and spiritual development. Valerie Rickel, its founder and creator, was deeply touched and inspired by her father, an artist and philosopher, and in his wisdom, creativity, and spirituality, she found the seed for both her web site and a series of books.

The passing of her father and mother and the traumatic events of 9/11 all proved to be catalyzing events from which were born Valerie's passionate interest in soulful living and her intense search for life's meaning. Deeply committed to the opportunities her web site and books have opened to her, Valerie's mission is to share her passion for soulful living and inspire and enhance the lives of others.

Entering its' fifth year on the World Wide Web, SoulfulLiving. com has won accolades from the media and has been featured in numerous print publications, including *Health and Fitness Magazine, Health* magazine, the *Los Angeles Business Journal,* and *Gospel Today* magazine. As Meg Sanders, author of the book, *The Good Web Guide to Mind, Body & Spirit*, writes, "As soon as the homepage appears, you know you're in the hands of professionals. . . . Elegant, erudite, ambitious and sincere, this site sets the standard, but we've seen few others that even come close."

# Living Your Truth

While I was growing up, my father often said, "The Truth cannot be told." This was one of his favorite expressions, and it brought me to one of my own: "*Your* Truth cannot be told." Why not? you ask, and I reply, *Because our Truth is our Highest Good, our Heart, our authentic inner knowing.* It is unique to each of us. It is our special gift, our Light, the reason we are here. Our Truth is not a Truth that "can be told" to us by another. It is a Truth that we each must find for ourselves.

Several months after my father's death, I heard my own Truth—the wisdom in my Heart—calling me. I found myself spending every free moment, day and night, dreaming of and creating a web site community focused on spirituality and personal growth. It was to be called SoulfulLiving.com. My soul had been "called." It was one of those things that I knew I could not not do. Two years later, when my mother and nephew became very ill (their illnesses were unrelated) and were hospitalized at the same time, it became clear to me that life is too short to do anything less in life than what you are most passionate about. I found the courage to leave my full-time job, an eight-year career in marketing and public relations in the shopping center industry, and devote myself full-time to SoulfulLiving.com.

It hasn't always been a smooth journey. There were times when people close to me were critical of the work I've chosen to do. They said I was crazy for leaving my comfortable, stable career, and I have to admit it: sometimes I allowed their suggestions to get under my skin and invade my psyche. I am still growing and gaining wisdom, however, and now I understand that it has been those very criticisms that helped me to gain the firm conviction that I am doing exactly the work I was put here on earth to do. *I know deeply in my Heart that I am living my Truth.* SoulfulLiving. com is my special purpose—my gift, my Light.

Always remember that your Heart—your Truth—will never lead you astray. Let the Light of your Heart guide your way.

# SUSAN EMILY PITT

**Susan Emily Pitt,** our cover designer, is a metaphysician, visionary artist and author of *Aspects of Self - the Game of Life*. Twice paralyzed, a foreign-exchange student in USA, wife of thirty-three years, mother, grandmother and restaurateur, being a farmer's wife in a war zone, fashion-designer, book illustrator and animated film-maker, have gifted Susan with the ability to envision a vast array of energies. Exploring the hidden potentials of the Dreamer within each one of us, she paints your individual 'Soul Portrait' for inspiration, using symbols of the natural world to express the rich tapestry of your life. You can contact her at *http://www.soulportraits.com* or at susanemily@allafrica.net.

Human beings, like the finest gemstones, contain innumerable facets. Each one of these presents a different one of our 'faces' to the world, and in turn allows us to see things from that particular perspective. The problem with we humans is that we tend to like our comfort zones, and tend to get stuck using only a few of these possible facets. This may be due to conditioning, force of circumstance etc, with the unfortunate result that we often may either not perceive, or dream, of reaching our full potential.

By allowing these hidden energies to re-enter our consciousness, we unlock potentials which have long lain dormant or been completely hidden from us. I believe that the symbols of the natural world, by which man used to be guided through life, have slowly, over time, been forgotten on a conscious level, though not on any other level. What has happened is that we have forgotten how to read the symbols we are presented with daily, which could help to give us direction and empower us to Self-esteem, Self-reliance and fulfillment of Self.

In abandoning our dreams and submitting ourselves to the beliefs of others - by forgetting the natural magic that is all around us and which is available to nurture and empower us every step of our way, we impose unnecessary limitations on ourselves. You are NOT simply your body, nor your personality, but so very much more. We often hide our Selves out of fear of our own beauty and power.

So, I invite you. Come dance the dream with me. Dust off your cobwebs; come and explore the not-so-mundane world we live in and see life truly through your mystic Dreamer's eyes.

How do you see yourself and how do you interpret what you see? Do you see past the surface image to the true beauty of who you are inside, your radiant Self? Sometimes we are so caught up in the everyday hurly-burly of what we call 'making a living' that we forget that we are not merely our bodies, nor behavior, nor our thoughts, but something very much grander.. With an image before you of the magnificent being you truly are, no longer would you have to remain stuck in the frozen beliefs of who you thought you were.

---

*"When the artist is alive in any person, whatever his kind of work may be, he becomes an inventive, searching, daring, self-expressive creature. He becomes interesting to other people. He disturbs, upsets, enlightens, and opens ways for a better understanding. Where those who are not artists are trying to close the book, he opens it and shows there are still more pages possible."*

~ **Robert Henri,** *The Art Spirit*

---

What is a Soul Portrait? It is a unique map to the treasure of your hidden self. Once I connect and become sensitive to your vibrations, I can sense the energies surrounding you, which have an essence similar to your own and thus express who you really are. Each feeling I get has a unique signature, which matches a specific symbol or object. Once I interpret these, I begin to assemble all the symbols on the page around a picture of the person. Each picture will have a very definite arrangement of objects, colors, Runic symbols, sometimes sacred geometry and numerology, possibly the angelic hierarchy and even past lives which are representative of that persons' soul. At times the right arrangement comes quickly and sometimes it takes a lot longer. Often I will just have finished penciling it on to the paper when another object or two will come along and insist on being included. Each symbol will give you more insight into who, what and where you truly are. The portraits are always uplifting and joyful and reflect your true soul, beauty and power, offering symbolic clues to your own map of life. It's a bit like a treasure map, where the treasure is your hidden Self.

# GUY FINLEY

Guy Finley is one of today's brightest voices in the field of self-realization showing men and women how to find a life of freedom, enduring fulfillment, and true purpose. Nightingale-Conant, the world's largest producer of motivational books on tape, calls Guy Finley *"one of the leading experts at the forefront of human potential."* Barnes and Noble states, *"Guy Finley has helped millions live fuller, more peaceable lives."*

Director of the non-profit Life of Learning Foundation, Guy is the best-selling author of more than twenty books and tape albums on self-liberation. These include: ***The Secret of Letting Go, Design Your Destiny, Freedom from the Ties that Bind, The Intimate Enemy, Lost Secrets of Prayer, Seeker's Guide to Self-Freedom,*** and ***Let Go and Know Peace.*** His works have sold over a million copies worldwide and have been translated into 11 languages. Guy has been featured on over 400 radio and TV talk shows including Larry King Live, Sally Jesse Raphael, CNN, PBS, Entertainment Tonight, Coast-to-Coast Live with Art Bell, NPR, David Essel Alive, and the Wisdom Channel. His writings have been featured as "Today's Pick" in USA Today and his work is recommended by doctors and counselors. Guy presents more than 150 seminars each year on self-liberation.

*"Letting Go with Guy Finley,"* a series of videotaped inner life talks, appears on cable channels across the nation. His talks also air weekly on *www.wisdomradio.com.* Guy offers a monthly Internet chat room classroom to students worldwide on his award-winning website ***www.guyfinley.com.***

# LET LOVE LIFT YOUR WORLD

Every conscious act of Love lifts the world, so that each genuine expression of kindness embraces and elevates all willing souls. While every angry thought lashes the soul, infecting the world with its bitterness until the will of what is dark within that hatefulness crushes the unwitting soul, causing her to lose her precious little Light.

**For further understanding. . .**

**Going Beyond the Limitations of Thoughts**

When it comes to our spiritual being, every moment serves to either nourish within us the inherent freedom of Real Life, or it acts to negate this grand possibility and keeps us prisoners of our own unconsciousness. And if we had eyes to see into the secret realm of Self that sits behind the determining reality of our existence, we would witness therein that each of our thoughts, either consciously or carelessly embraced, forms within us the cells of our spiritual being. These building blocks of our supersensual "self" structure are what we call our experience of life, so that even as we think what we want to be, so are we made to become this self by the nature of these very thoughts.

But these insights reveal only a fraction of the story of our whole life possibility. Our thoughts, like all energetic life forms, attract to themselves natures like themselves. The thoughts of a fellow not only flock together, but also seek and are sought out by similar invisible creatures. The implications of this discovery all point to one imperative: Our first action, our first choice in life - regardless of the circumstances life has put us in - must be to come awake within ourselves. We must work to be conscious of the nature of whatever thoughts and feelings are running through us . . . and for good reason. Here is why such self-watchfulness is so vital to our spiritual well being.

Whether we are conscious of it or not, our prevailing sense of self is largely determined by the nature of our invisible interior relationship with these widely varying mental and emotional states. For upon whatever our attention is given, it is there that we stand inwardly, and whatever the actual nature of this ground may be - for the strength or shakiness of it - we share in that level of life.

Serious students of the inner-life oftentimes ask, "What steps can I take to begin putting these principles to work in my day-to-day life? What specific things can I do to begin making this upward journey?"

**Look In The Right Direction**

To look for tropical fruit in the open arctic is a waste of time. If you wish to see soaring birds, you need to lift your eyes from the ground. The lesson is this: without knowing *where to look*, you can't expect to find what you're looking for. Never is this truer than when it comes to looking for why you're *still looking* for ways to be stronger than those situations, which continue to overcome you. The problem is you're looking in the wrong places. The solution is to turn around and look in a new direction.

Whenever we find ourselves feeling angry or worried in some way, we always ask certain familiar questions. But these personal inquiries are not what they seem. They are really *answers disguised as questions*; not actually *asking* anything, rather secretly confirming that we know where to look -- for who -- or what -- is to blame for our shaky feelings. And in this same moment where we're able to name the cause of our conflict-filled feelings, there's something else that's secretly confirmed which seals this unsuspected self deception: We're sure the source of what's making us shake, or ache, rests *outside* of us. And it's *this* unquestioned assumption, which keeps us looking in the wrong direction; where we remain a perpetual victim in search of victory never found. Now here's the right direction in which to look:

When faced with any shaky, achy feeling, *look within*. Just ignore those pointed thoughts telling you where the blame falls. Let your attention fall back upon yourself instead by learning to *ask your own questions* about your situation. This is the only way to see that the real source of those painful tremors is not outside of you, but that it dwells within one of a hundred false ideas about yourself that you've come to believe are true. And when you see that you've abandoned yourself to a nature, which can never be anything higher than a blame-inflamed victim, real Self Victory follows. Now, to help you learn how to look in the right direction, consider the set of special questions below created just for this special study.

1. **Stop asking in secret defeat:**
   *When will these unpleasant circumstances in my life finally change?*

   **Start consciously asking:**
   *What is it in me that that only feels worthwhile as long as circumstances warrant it?*

   **Or:** *What is it in me that only knows how to meet life's events at their own level?*

2. **Stop asking in secret defeat:**
   *Why can't you see that you're wrong?*

   **Start consciously asking:**
   *What is it in me that just doesn't feel right until it's certain someone else knows it is?*

   **Or:** *What is it in me that only knows how right it is by the measure of its anger?*

3. **Stop asking in secret defeat:**
   *Where is this scary situation going to lead?*

   **Start consciously asking:**
   *What is it in me that can only hear what fear has to say about a possible event?*

   **Or:** *What is it in me that has no direction in life outside of being told where it's headed?*

**For extra benefits:** *Each day, at a point and time designated by you, go on a one-hour retreat <u>with nothing.</u> Find a place where you can be by yourself and meet the hour alone and unknown. Spend this personal time without bringing anything <u>known</u> into it with you. Just be you, whatever that brings with it. And it bears mentioning that you can't fail at this exercise. To attempt it is to venture into the unknown. If you'll do this much, the Truth will take care of the rest.*

# TEN WAYS TO MAKE GOD'S LIFE YOUR OWN

1.  *Remembering* to remember God when doing needful business with another person reminds you that is it impossible to serve two masters and hope to succeed -- but that Real Success comes to you when you see this truth.

2.  *Remembering* to remember God when someone praises you keeps you from forgetting that the light you have shown to win the applause is only a gifted reflection.

3.  *Remembering* to remember God while condemning yourself reminds you that you are too harsh to be your own judge and that there's a Higher Court of Appeal whose verdict is the standing order to start your life all over.

4.  *Remembering* to remember God when taking your meals will help keep you from abandoning yourself to that nature which always abandons you after its consumed its desire.

5.  *Remembering* to remember God in your travels reveals that your dwelling place is always where your heart is and that no place is better or worse than what you bring into it.

6.  *Remembering* to remember God while being lashed about by your own storming thoughts and feelings makes it evident that you do not have to stand out in the rain.

7.  *Remembering* to remember God in the face of a fear or loss reminds you that you've a choice in what you cling to, and that letting go of what is pulling you down is the same as turning in a higher, happier direction.

8.  *Remembering* to remember God in the midst of a conflict helps to clarify that you can go on fighting over what is impermanent – or – fight for your spiritual freedom by walking away from the compulsive need to win.

9.  *Remembering* to remember God when doing things you wish you didn't have to do ~ will connect you with Something always content to be where it is ~ always pleased with Who it is.

10. *Remembering* to remember God when doubting that remembering God does you any good ~ places your need for the Truth above your own suspicion that you may lack sincerity ~ is the beginning of True Spiritual Sincerity.

© Guy Finley

# If Only

There are some – deep of faith
And know of one Supreme above all
Who, caring for the sparrow's fall,
Needs only heart of prayer
To bring forth things beyond our ken.

But my friend, a man of substance, self-made and
strong of will needs more:
"If only I could see a miracle ~ then I would Believe."

So one lazy, hazy summer's day
We sat on grassy bank beneath the shade of
whispering trees
Beside a quietly running stream
And talked, as men sometimes will,
Of deep philosophies, great thoughts, and
cabbages and kings.

Idly he plucked a blade of new-grown grass
Not yet full with summer's life
And touched the tiny seeds barely seen
Of blades yet to be born a thousand, no, a
thousand thousand generations hence
Yet holding pattern from before the time
That man has been upon this earth
His voice was soft in query while he twirled the
seeds, slow in thought
"If only I could see a miracle ~ then I would
believe."

We sat in idle warmth, a dragonfly
On iridescent flashing wings
Passed nearby on its endless quest
For purpose yet to be fulfilled
Myriad rainbows cascaded in the path through
sunlight streaks
Great purple eyes ~ what kind of world do such
things see?
Again that murmur,
"If only I could see a miracle ~ then I would believe."

I stretched, face down, cheek on cooling earth
And there, darting in the stream
Were tiny fingerlings of who knows what breed
Passing on their way to greater deeps.
Yet sometime hence they would return,
Full, and strong and great.
To play their part and die to help their kind
survive
An endless play of cycles ~ life and death
Repeated since before time was.
As I watched, a tiny ant ran on my hand.
Could it sense my life?  Or was I to it
Just another stone or monumental branch to slow
its path?
Could such as these have weighty thoughts like
ours?
About universal truths and worlds beyond the
stars?
What could they know?  They couldn't – could
they?
My train of thought was broken ~ my friend once
more
"If only I could see a miracle ~ then I would
believe."

A cooling breeze, with summer's gentle hand
Blew across our face
Who knows from what Saharan waste
Or frigid Arctic cold it may have sprung?
Surely this same breeze had touched
a myriad score of other men, and more.
The earth's good trees, the forest floors
And all the world's great oceans
Lifting water to the skies
Passing hot or cold, wet or dry
In concert with some mighty Chemist's plan,
To give survival to all who held that
greatest Chemist's gift ~ life itself.
When suddenly I heard the words
"If only I could see a miracle
then I would believe."

We leaned back against the great tree trunk
This tree, with such graceful arms
and thankful shade
I touched a pod, now old and dead
Yet from such as this it may have sprung
Countless summers long before.
And I thought of other trees, dwarfing this,
Starting life before man walked
And still alive, undaunted,
With promise from their ancient past
For futures yet to come
And in this seed?
Were we then all part of one great Truth?
I was interrupted with a sigh:
My friend,
"If only I could see a miracle
then I would believe."


The day now gone, we slowly wandered home,
My friend still deep in quest
"How I envy them," he said,
Those who pray to one Supreme
Those who know there is a Power over all
"If only ~ if only ~ I could see a miracle
then I would believe."


And the swallows, flying low,
Dipped wings blue glazed with evening's beauty
As if in silent tribute to his plea.

© Dr. Charles Parry

# WAYNE W. DYER, PH.D

**Dr. Wayne W. Dyer,** affectionately called the "father of motivation" by his fans, is one of the most widely known and respected people in the field of self-empowerment. He became a well-known author with his bestselling book, *Your Erroneous Zones*, and has gone on to write many other self-help classics, including *Meditations for Manifesting, Staying on the Path, Your Sacred Self, Everyday Wisdom*, and *You'll See It When You Believe It.*

Despite his childhood spent in orphanages and foster homes, Dr. Dyer, who has a doctorate in counseling psychotherapy, has overcome many obstacles to make his dreams come true. Today he spends much of his time showing others how to do the same. His latest Hay House titles include: *Wisdom of the Masters, Creating Your World the Way You Really Want It to Be* (with Deepak Chopra), *How to Get What You Really, Really, Really, Really Want, Inner Peace Cards, There Is a Spiritual Solution To Every Problem, Dr. Wayne Dyer's Ten Secret's For Success and Inner Peace*, and his new release *Getting in the Gap: Making Conscious Contact with God Through Meditation.*

**Treat Yourself As If You Already Are
What You'd Like to Be**

t is that you envision for yourself – no matter
ty or impossible it may seem to you right
encourage you to begin acting as if what you
me is already your reality. This is a wonderful
otion the forces that will collaborate with you
ams come true. To activate the creative forces
in your life, you must go to the unseen world,
d your form. Here is where what doesn't exist for
ld of form will be created. You might think of it
form, you receive in-formation. When you move
eceive in-spiration. It is this world of inspiration
e you to access anything that you would like to
ife.

## ...ns to Become Inspired

Some of the most significant advice I've ever read was written
more than 2,000 years ago by an ancient teacher named
Patanjali. He instructed his devotees to become inspired. You
may recall that the word inspire originates from the words *in* and
*spirit*. Patanjali suggested that inspiration involves a mind that
transcends all limitations, thoughts that break all their bonds, and
a consciousness that expands in every direction. Here is how you
can become inspired.

Place your thoughts on what it is you'd like to have or become —
an artist, a musician, a computer programmer, a dentist, or
whatever. In your thoughts, begin to picture yourself having
the skills to do these things. No doubts. Only a knowing.

The more you see yourself as what you'd like to become, the
more inspired you are. The dormant forces that Patanjali
described come alive, and you discover that you're a greater
person than you ever dreamed yourself to be. Imagine that -
dormant forces that were dead or nonexistent, springing into
being and collaborating with you as a result of your becoming
inspired and acting as if what you want is already here!

By having the courage to declare yourself as already being where you want to be, you will almost force yourself to act in a new, exciting, and spiritual fashion. You can also apply this principle to areas other than your chosen vocation. If you're living a life of scarcity, and all of the nice things that many people have are not coming your way, perhaps it's time to change your thinking and act as if what you enjoy having is already here.

There is a silent agreement between you and God in which you discreetly work in harmony with the forces of the universe to make your dreams become a reality. This involves a knowing on your part that success and inner peace are your birthright; that you are a child of God; and as such, you're entitled to a life of joy, love, and happiness. Then begin acting as if these things were already your reality. As an artist, your vision allows you to draw, to visit art museums, to talk with famous artists, and to immerse yourself in the art world. In other words, you begin to act as an artist in all aspects of your life. In this way, you're getting out in front of yourself and taking charge of your own destiny at the same time that you're cultivating inspiration.

## WHY MEDITATE

When we meditate, we begin to still the mind. As we get more and more adept at moving into inner silence, we come to know the peace of God in our entire being. We intuitively seek union with our generating Source. Silence, or meditation, is the path to that center: We can make conscious contact with God, transcend the power that is only available to us when we're connected to the Source. This is what I call getting in the gap. It's where we create, manifest, heal, live and perform at a miraculous level. The gap is the powerful silence we can access through meditation. By entering the elusive gap between our thoughts, we can access the stillness that may have been unattainable in other meditation attempts.

Our ultimate reason for meditating is to get in the gap where we enter the sacred space and know the unlimited power of our

Source. Psalm 46:10 says: "Be still, and know that I am God." To know is to banish all doubt. Being still in meditation can take us to that awareness. But if you've tried meditating previously, what you're more likely to know is that your thoughts won't be still.

I find it helpful to think of my mind as a pond. The surface of the pond is similar to my mental chatter. On the surface of the pond are the disturbances. Here there are storms, debris, freezing and thawing, all on the surface. Beneath the pond surface, there is relative stillness. Here it is quiet and peaceful. If, as has been said, it's true that we have approximately 60,000 separate, often disconnected, thoughts during the day, then our mind is like a pond that's full of whitecaps from a choppy breeze. But beneath that surface chatter is the gap where we can know God and gain the unlimited power of reconnecting to our Source.

Mediating is a way of quieting our chatterbox thoughts and swimming below the surface. This is where we can be still and know (not know about) God. If we have approximately 60,000 thoughts every day, then in all of our waking hours, it's unlikely that we ever get to the point where there's any space between our thoughts. How could we? With one thought leading to the next, either rationally connected or otherwise, there's simply no time or place to get into the gap between our thoughts. Yet it's precisely in that gap that the magic and the infinite possibilities await us.

The practice of meditation takes us on a fabulous journey into the gap between our thoughts, where all the advantages of a peaceful, stress-free, healthier, fatigue-free life are available, but are simply side benefits. The paramount reason for doing this soul-nourishing mediation practice is to get in the gap between our thoughts and make conscious contact with the creative energy of life itself. But this is a choice that's entirely the responsibility of each individual. We have the potential to be instruments of the highest good for all concerned and to be miracle workers in our own lives.

As you engage in prolonged meditation sessions, and experience what you bring back to the material world, you will know God. . . . and you'll know why you choose to meditate.

# ASOKA SELVARAJAH, Ph.D

**Asoka Selvarajah** is an active writer/researcher on personal growth and spirituality, and the author of "The 7 Golden Secrets To Knowing Your Higher Self". His work helps people achieve their full potential, deepen their understanding of mystical truth, and discover their soul's purpose. Asoka holds a Ph.D. in Nuclear Physics, and is a former Investment Banker. You can visit him at http://www.aksworld.com where he offers you his FREE 14-Day Life Breakthrough Course, and welcomes your feedback via his Discussion Board.

# THE SECRET OF THE MASTERS — YOURS!

Aleister Crowley made a profound observation that I remembered from the first time I read it. He pointed out that the one thing Jesus Christ, the Buddha, Mohammed, Moses and all other great spiritual teachers have in common is that they retreated into the wilderness prior to receiving and delivering their great revelations. Apart from this, their lives and teachings were totally different. So too were the people they preached to and the messages they taught.

Jesus was baptized by John and promptly disappeared into the desert for forty days and forty nights. The Buddha escaped from the samsaric slumber of the royal palace in which he was born, and meditated under a Bodhi Tree for many years before enlightenment came. Alone, Moses disappeared to the top of Mount Sinai and received the Ten Commandments, and more, from the burning bush of God. The Prophet Mohammed spent much time in a lonely cave at night in the hills outside Mecca before he received the Koran from the Angel Gabriel.

Silence. Retreat. A Wilderness Experience. Communing deeply within. This is the X factor. This inner retreat is the only spiritually distinctive thing about these people at all. Virgin birth apart, the life of Jesus prior to this isolation is hardly even discussed in the Gospels. The Buddha was one of many Indian princes. You couldn't have picked Mohammed out in a crowd. And Moses, though an accomplished magician at the time, and leader of a nation of homeless and hungry, had his best days ahead of him.

When they returned from their periods of silence and solitude, they came with FIRE! The flames of that fire gave light to the world. The truths they revealed differed markedly, according to their own times, as well as the history and traditions of the people they taught. But all shared divine revelations.

From this dramatic comparison of the lives of the Spiritual Masters, we get a strong sense of how to conduct our own spiritual retreats. Through meditation we can truly break through the barriers and blocks that prevent us from realizing who we really are and finding our own life's destiny. If you need any more persuading, consider the following from some of the greatest minds ever known:

*All of man's problems stem from his inability to sit quietly with himself.*

– Pascal

*You can't teach anybody anything; only make them realize the answers are already inside them.*

– Galileo

*When you go into the space of nothingness, everything becomes known.*

– Buddha

*You can never learn anything that you did not already know.*

– Aristotle

*The Kingdom of Heaven is within you.*

– Jesus Christ

An old story relates that the Gods debated as to where to hide their wealth of wisdom and spiritual power. They finally settled on hiding it deep within Man himself. They knew man would look for it everywhere in the universe except within!

Thus, if you wish to make progress in anything--spiritual, material, or even financial--the place to start is within. This is where the Inner Genius lays, the Higher Self, the Power of God. Spend time with yourself in contemplation. Wait upon that inner voice. Drop your preconceptions. "Be still and know that I Am God."

The truly wise person knows that inner victory must always precede outer. There are no shortcuts. It takes time and patience. It is out of sorts with the ways of the world, which is precisely its power. You may not even know how to begin or what to expect. Just begin. Schedule regular time for meditation. All questions will be answered in time. By You!

# THE MEDITATION KEY

Meditation is rightly considered an excellent practice for spiritual and personal growth. It is easy to begin, and yet there is endless scope for the accomplished practitioner to go ever deeper. Hence, a meditation practice suited to your personal needs is highly recommended.

If you have never meditated before, and are unsure where to begin, here are a few simple pointers. You are recommended to consult more detailed books, or a live meditation teacher, as soon as you are able.

## Establish a definite place and time

Developing a regular time is important. You want to build this practice into a regular habit, and not leave it as a once in a while diversion, when you have "nothing better to do". Make an appointment with yourself to do this EVERY day, at least once a day. It does not have to be very long: even fifteen minutes is quite adequate when you are getting started.

## Reserve a space in your home

A separate room would be perfect. However, if you cannot do this, then at least try to reserve a small area of one room for this purpose. You could even go outside if necessary. Wherever possible, try to select a place where you are unlikely to be disturbed, and which is quiet. Highly experienced meditators can practice in the middle of a busy street. However, when you are starting out, some peace and quiet is essential.

## Seat yourself ~ make comfort balanced with alertness the priority

You want to find a position you can remain in for some time without excessive fidgeting. It doesn't have to be a lotus posture, unless this works for you. Simply sitting on the floor cross-legged, or even sitting upright in a chair, works fine. Avoid lying on your back, as you are likely to drift off to sleep. Your eyes should either be closed, or else only slightly open, with heavy eyelids.

Here are two simple processes to commence with, but which can stay with you for the rest of your life. Do not be deceived by their apparent simplicity. They are deep, powerful and highly purifying to the mind.

## Follow your breathing

This is a technique recommended by the Buddha himself, and by countless teachers after him. With eyes closed, you focus your attention ever more carefully on the rising and falling of your breath. Throughout this process, you should be breathing from your abdomen, which rises and falls with every inhalation and exhalation. One variation is to follow the breath in through your nostrils, then down into your lungs, being aware of them filling up, and then out through your mouth as your lungs deflate. Hence, you follow the path of your breath through your body.

Another variation is to focus solely on your nose, and actually feel the passage of your breath through it alone. If you do, you will feel your nostrils cool slightly as you inhale, and warm slightly as you exhale.

## Be aware of the passage of your thoughts.

You will find that thoughts will intrude anyway during your meditation periods. So why not make some positive use of them? In this practice, the purity of your consciousness is like the clear blue sky across which your thoughts, like clouds, arise and disappear. As you work with this process, you will come to realize that it is not really you who is thinking. Rather, thoughts seem to arise by themselves within the mind, from a wholly different source.

In this latter practice, it is important to not get caught up with the train of thought and get carried away. Rather, you are playing the part of the detached observer, watching your thoughts, rather as you might watch the motion of waves upon the ocean.

What happens if, during either the breathing meditation, or the observation of your thoughts, you happen to get carried away with daydreaming? That is fine. As soon as you become aware of it, simply return to the meditation.

As you continue, you will find your practice improving. You will be able to meditate for longer. Your mind will become more focused, and ever less distracted and carried away with thinking. You will experience tremendous mental, physical, and spiritual benefits. Indeed, you will carry this happy mental state out of the formal session and into your life. Meditation is the foundation upon which you can build a happy and spiritually enriched existence. Try it for yourself and see.

# Deepak Chopra, M.D.

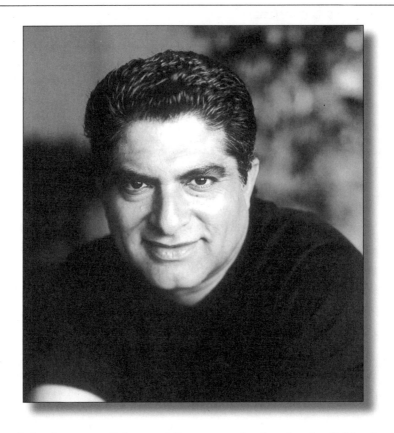

Acknowledged as one of the world's greatest leaders in the field of mind-body medicine, **Deepak Chopra, M.D.** is known worldwide for his published works. He has been published on every continent, and in dozens of languages. More than twenty million copies of Deepak's books have been sold worldwide, and include *Grow Longer, Live Longer: 10 Steps to Reverse Aging; How to Know God: The Soul's Journey into the Mystery of Mysteries, Perfect Health; Ageless Body, Timeless Mind; The Seven Spiritual Laws of Success; The Return of Merlin,* and *The Path to Love. The Chopra Center Herbal Handbook; The Complete Mind / Body Program For Achieving and Maintaining Your Ideal Weight; Restful Sleep: The Complete Mind / Body Program For Overcoming Insomnia; Quantum Healing: Exploring the Frontiers of Mind / Body Medicine and Creating Health. Popular audio books and CD-ROMS include Magical Mind, Magical Body; The Higher Self; Journey to the Boundless;* and *The Wisdom Within.* Many know him from his work with PBS, which includes *Body, Mind and Soul: The Mystery and The Magic,* and *The Way of the Wizard, Alchemy* and *The Crystal Cave.*

Dr. Chopra maintains an extensive website with information on many topics, including The Chopra Foundation which, through The Alliance for the New Humanity project (conducted in partnership with the Oscar Arias Foundation) is dedicated to creating a peaceful world. For more information or to participate in one of the Alliance's Peace Cells go to *http://www.chopra.com.*

If a man could find the Banyan Tree in India that is said, by the ancient sages, to grant any wish to the person sitting under it, he would have to be careful. Too many good wishes have gone awry, leaving evil in their wake. Let us suppose that the man knows all about the ravaged rain forests, the hole in the ozone layer, and the stockpiled warheads. He doesn't want to assign blame for these horrors. He realizes instead how ultimately his future is tied up with everyone else's.

How could he possibly make a wish only for himself? He would want to desire a world that everyone can share and that poses a problem. There is no single happiness that applies to everyone. Looking up from his seat under the Banyan Tree, he would observe the bullock carts carrying farmers who have not changed their way of life for centuries. Perhaps a black Mercedes overtakes them, and the impatient industrialist inside scowls as he drives the carts out of his way. A jet breaks the silence overhead, scaring up a flock of mites who have nested in the same tree since man first appeared.

*"My country has been enriched by the contributions of more than a million Indian Americans, which includes Dr. Deepak Chopra, the pioneer of alternative medicine."*

**President William Clinton**

How to satisfy the needs of the rich and the poor, the educated and the illiterate, the virtuous and the not so virtuous? How to permit man his ingenuity and creativity without laying waste to the green Planet, and the animals, and the birds who accept their existence upon it so innocently? The wisher imagines the hateful conflicts that would arise from even the most benignly conceived future.

But, he must wish for some better world! The one we now inhabit contains too much destruction. We did not put the destructive power into nature. As a primal force, destruction is linked to creation, and is just as necessary. But we drove it beyond some invisible limit that was not foreseen. The troubling truth is that human creativity, far more than our greed and hate, tipped the balance of nature. The same DNA gave birth to the rain forests, the animals, and man himself.

Through man, the intelligence of life kept pushing its way into the future; it discovered how to unleash any force in nature, and at that point something broke down. We are living in someone else's idea of a brave new world, as it was wished for by past generations. Why has man's DNA turned against its own interest, threatening to topple everything? "Ignorance," our wisher thinks, "all this evil has come out of the potential for good – it is sheer ignorance." In that thought, he would have the seed of his wish. The only survivable future is one in which ignorance has been abolished. Man is not a cancer let loose on the face of the earth; his DNA is the DNA of all life. Its interests have been safeguarded by nature for 600 million years, and its basic atoms have been protected from destruction from the Big Bang.

---

*Time Magazine heralds Deepak Chopra as one of the top 100 heroes and icons of the century, and credits him as "the poet-prophet of alternative medicine."*
                                        *Time Magazine,* June 1999.

---

What we fail to grasp is a way to return to the broad, shining river of evolution that has sustained us for eons already. A return implies a path. This path is hard to conceive of, unfortunately, since there is nowhere to go. We are already in nature; the forests, however ravaged, are obeying the same laws as before. The plankton and whales and seals, which we devastate, have no way to live other than the way they have always lived. The root of the damaged world is in our interpretation. We got this world because it suits our vision of ourselves. From one grim Roman saying, "Man is the wolf to man," we can see the origin of war, degradation, prejudice, rivalry, and hate. The same holds true for any other evil in the world. It is the visible evidence of an invisible weakness or fault in us.

Certainly he is right the path of ignorance begins and ends in our minds. "To restore nature," our wisher concludes, "I must change my own nature." At this point I believe we must take a leap and believe in resilience and final goodness of the life in us. To change human nature seems like the most impossible task of all unless this mounting nightmare has all been a mistake. The

Upanishads, the most ancient record of man's self-knowledge, declare, "Of bliss these creatures were conceived, in bliss they live, and into bliss they will merge again." The horrors of history may not confirm these words, but man's aspirations do.

The collected wisdom for returning to man's true nature takes the name Ayur-Veda in Sanskrit, which means "the science of life." Conventional Veda has been interpreted as a system of medicine, but we must understand that in the broadest terms. Health, as Ayur-Veda aims to uphold it, means not just a sane mind in a sane body, (the classic ideal in the West), but a full expansion of man's inner potential. "I am the universe" is the primary intuition of a healthy man. The ideals of love, compassion, and freedom are fully alive in him; his comprehension of the human situation includes all life around him.

If I were the wisher under the Banyan Tree, I would wish for every person to recover his own true inner nature. In seed form, this is already occurring. The movement to spread Ayur-Veda to every country has been thriving for more than a decade. (The direct inspiration came from Maharishi Mahesh Yogi, the founder of Transcendental Meditation, who revived this ancient knowledge in the early 1980's).

Ayur-Veda began in India, but its essence is universal, and the kind of future I foresee will have many Ayur-Vedas in it, as each person and each nation finds its own path back to the stream of evolution. It is not that we must perform the heroic task of saving nature.

The same pulsation of life flows through the whole world, emanating from the gods or God. That unimaginable force created the galaxies and at the same time preserves the most fragile mountain flower. All around us life gushes forth and meets itself coming back, curving in joy onto itself and leaping in jubilation at its own infinite strength. We are part of this stream too. We issued from it, and our destiny continues to ride its crest.

# Seeing Beyond

The literal meaning of transcending is "going beyond," and at moments of clarity it is possible for anyone to be aware that reality isn't confined to the five senses. Peak experiences open up windows to spirit. Yet "going beyond" is not an accurate description of the experience of transcending, since there is no distance to cover; spirit never leaves us, it is only overlooked. This practice trains you to stop overlooking the spirit and love that surround you, waiting to be noticed.

Although it means "going beyond," a better way to describe transcending is "seeing beyond." What can you see beyond the apparently solid facade of life, the constant flow of time, the limitations of space, and the laws of cause and effect? If the answer is very little, the reason is that your perception has not been trained for such vision. Yet every day contains clues of the second reality we all inhabit, which is timeless, unbounded, causeless, and intimately tied to our needs on the path to love.

First examine the following list to determine if you have experienced these sorts of clues:

1. In the midst of danger or crisis, have you suddenly had the feeling of being completely safe and protected?
2. Have you ever been with someone who was dying and felt a sense of peace or a coolness in the air when the moment of passing came?
3. Have you known someone who recovered from an "incurable" illness?
4. Have you prayed and had your prayer answered?
5. Have you ever witnessed a soft light around another person or yourself?
6. Have you ever asked for silent guidance or the answer to a dilemma and received it?
7. When looking at a sunset, a full moon, or something of great natural beauty, have you felt yourself expand as if you were no longer enclosed within the physical limits of your body?
8. Have you experienced a silencing of your mind, perhaps just before going to sleep or on first waking up?

9. Have you felt a loving presence when you most needed it?
10. Do you ever hear an inner voice you feel you can absolutely rely on? (This voice doesn't have to speak in words; it can also be a strong feeling or intuition.)
11. Have you felt wonder at the sight of a newborn child?

This isn't a quiz. You aren't trying to answer yes to as many questions as possible, but if you did say yes to any of them, pick the one that resonated most for you. Let us say it was the first one: feeling a sudden sense of safety and protection in the midst of crisis or danger. Close your eyes and put yourself back into that situation; see all the details of where you were, who you were with, what time it was and so on.

Try to relive the moment, but instead of being the person who was reacting at that moment, ask to be given a larger perspective. Ask to see the meaning of what was happening, and request that the meaning be as specific as possible. Take a deep breath and listen to whatever response comes. Now interpret your answer. Do any of the following meanings come through?

I am loved. I am safe. A part of myself watches over me. I know. I am. The light is with me. God is real. God is. Nothing is wrong. I am at peace. Things are OK. I can love. Everything is one. These are the messages love is trying to send you at every moment. Each is extremely simple yet eternally true.

You do not have to have an extraordinary or peak experience to receive such messages, but peak experiences do bring sudden clarity.

*Attune yourself to spirit, and it will speak to you in love.*

Spirit isn't a phenomenon; it is the whispered truth within a phenomenon. As such, spirit is gentle, it persuades by the softest touch. The messages never get louder, only clearer. If you have the slightest hint of communication from spirit, ask for clarification; look at the preceding list if you need to. At first the links to spirit may seem tenuous and fragile, but as you grow more confident you will find that your life is full of meaning, that every moment has an aspect that goes beyond if you have the vision to find it.

# KUMUDA REDDY, M.D.

**Dr. Kumuda Reddy**, Ayurvedic Medicine Expert, Author and Speaker, has been practicing medicine for thirty years. Her mission in life is to spread the knowledge of *Ayurveda*. She is a woman of great service and compassion who wants to help people lead lives of health and perfection.

Dr. Reddy has authored several books on Maharishi Vedic Medicine, including *Forever Healthy; For a Blissful Baby; Golden Transition; Conquering Chronic Disease* and other books on Ayurvedic Medicine. Dr. Reddy has also coauthored a book of stories from the Upanishads, entitled *All Love Flows to the Self,* and a series of children's stories called the *Timeless Wisdom Series*, based on traditional Indian stories that she first heard as a child on her grandmother's knee.

In addition to her life as a doctor and a writer, Dr. Reddy is a devoted wife and a mother. She lives in Bethesda, Maryland with her husband Janardhan Reddy, M.D. and fellow expert in Maharishi Vedic Medicine, and their three children, Sundeep, Hima, and Suma.

**Dr. Reddy can be contacted for consultation**
**at 877-589-0590**
**or visit her website**
*www.allhealthyfamily.com*

# Ayurveda

## The Essential Need

## of the Time

*Ayurveda* is truly universal. Although many people may be concerned that *Ayurveda* is only a branch of Indian philosophy it is, in fact, a truly universal system of medicine, which has withstood the test of time. The ancient texts of *Ayurveda* give the complete knowledge of diagnosis, prevention and treatment of every health concern there is and nothing is excluded.

*Ayurveda* is like the ocean where all the various streams of healing can merge and feel fulfilled. It is like the gardener who by nourishing the root also nurtures every branch of the tree because *Ayurveda* underlies all branches of holistic and conventional medicine. *Ayurveda* is so vast and comprehensive that it encompasses both. With *Ayurveda* the whole person is nurtured and nourished at the underlying level of consciousness.

Many people in these modern times are looking for answers to their health problems and they have several basic questions. They want to know what is *Ayurveda* and how does it work?

*Ayurveda* is a holistic and natural medicine that causes no negative side-effects and has many side-benefits. It is a system of prevention oriented natural healthcare that focuses on restoring balance at the deepest level of the mind and body. It treats everyone as an individual and treats the physical, mental, emotional and spiritual health. Health is the full expression of the body's inner intelligence. *Ayurveda* enlivens that inner intelligence, restoring balance and creating perfect health.

Ayurvedic medicine is different from modern medicine and other holistic practices because of its understanding of the consciousness that underlies everything. Every person is basically the same yet also unique. Everyone has a psychological, physical, and emotional makeup which requires different treatments as pertains to the individual because each person is different and prone to separate diseases.

### How are people different from each other?

In *Ayurveda* there are three main organizing principles that are found in every person, in nature, and other beings. These three governing principles are called *Vata*, *Pitta* and *Kapha doshas*. The *doshas* are the fundamental operators of every function in the mind and body but due to many factors they can go out of balance. Different people have different proportions of these *doshas*.

- *Vata* imbalances give rise to anxiety, fatigue, dry skin, constipation, joint and muscle pains, high blood pressure, painful irregular periods, insomnia, and other symptoms associated with *Vata*.

- *Pitta* imbalances give rise to irritability, anger, headaches, migraines, heavy periods, excess heat, graying and thinning hair, skin disorders, heartburn, ulcers, digestive problems, and other symptoms associated with *Pitta*.

- *Kapha* imbalances give rise to lethargy, asthma, allergies, sinusitis, congestive problems, obesity, fluid retention, depression, heart disease and other symptoms associated with *Kapha*.

### Does Ayurveda treat all problems in the same way?

If we just treat each patient in the same way then it is not effective. Two people can have the same root problem, but it can manifest in different ways. One person may have problems with digestion while another may have tension headaches or migraines. *Ayurveda* recognizes that each person is unique and needs a customized treatment.

### In what way does Ayurveda work in helping people with different problems?

Usually nobody comes to see me with one simple problem, such as fatigue. People have several symptoms at once. In conventional medicine we cannot understand the common source of these problems. The patient then goes to several specialists who treat each problem separately.

In *Ayurveda* we don't have to be so specialized because we treat the problem at its source without compromising the patient. Conventional medicine is good for crisis management, but not effective for chronic disorders. *Ayurveda* specializes in prevention and treatment of chronic disorders.

### How does one start with Ayurveda?

The first step is a comprehensive evaluation which results in individualized recommendations including,

- *Specific dietary recommendations*

- *Gentle therapeutic and rejuvenating herbal formulas which are extremely specific for the various imbalances*

- *Recommendations for daily and seasonal lifestyle patterns*

- *Specific types of exercise*

- *Stress reduction and development of full mental potential*

### What is Ayurvedic pulse diagnosis?

According to *Ayurveda*, the pulse contains all of the impulses of the physiology. The heart is constantly pumping blood throughout the body, 70 to 90 beats a minute. As the heart-pumped blood courses though the body, it's reverberating off every cell. That reverberation on a very quiet level is the impulse of how the physiology is working. By "reading" the pulse any disturbances in the *doshas* and blocks in the flow of biological intelligence can be detected at their most subtle levels. By analyzing the qualities of all the impulses in the pulse I can pinpoint precise imbalances and give immediate recommendations for restoring balance.

Within the three *doshas* are five subdivisions called *subdoshas*. The imbalances in the *subdoshas* give information about the specific areas of disease and areas of toxic buildup. Different imbalances of the *doshas* give rise to different disorders. By being able to gain immediate insight into what is going on in the physiology I can direct my questions to what factors might be causing the problem or problems. Then I can make very detailed recommendations.

The non-invasive approach of pulse diagnosis takes only a few minutes yet lets me know a great deal of information about the condition of the physiology. Such a simple tool gives me a deep understanding of the fundamental nature of my patient and the natural balance of his/her biological qualities that make him or her unique. In addition to my wide experience in *Ayurveda* I have a background in conventional medicine. This makes it easier for me to wean patients off of some or all of their conventional medications, and to incorporate the use of Ayurvedic diagnosis as a complement to those who need lab work and routine follow up.

*Ayurveda* goes beyond medicine to the ultimate goal of evolution which is the state of perpetual unshakable happiness that we call *ananda*, bliss or enlightenment. *Ayurveda* reminds us that the primary cause of disease is *pragya-aparadh*, which is the mistake of the intellect. The *pragya-aparadh* happens because we do not know our true nature. *Ayurveda* says that we are not only connected to our mind, body and environment but also we are the *atman*, or pure consciousness, or Self.

This Self is the source for all health and happiness. When we are disconnected from the Self because of ignorance then there is *pragya-aparadh*, which in turn leads to discomfort and disease at all levels. The ultimate goal of *Ayurveda* is to become healthy, happy and live a life of full potential.

*Ayurveda* recognizes that we are all cosmic and are related to everything in the cosmos (*Yatha pinda tatha Brahmanda*).

*As is the atom so is the cosmos.*

*As is the human mind so is the cosmic mind.*

*As is the human body so is the cosmic body.*

When we understand that the purpose of life is to evolve then we realize that this is the natural desire to seek the freedom of the Self through *Ayurveda*, which provides us with the knowledge of holistic health at all levels. *Ayurveda* is needed now more than ever because life has become more complex.

We need a holistic medicine which offers the totality in the prevention and treatment of all discomfort and disease. *Ayurveda* is the need of our time and the birthright of every human being. With *Ayurveda* you can begin anywhere, reach the goal where there is a clear health concern, and obtain the ultimate goal of enlightenment. *Now is the time to begin.*

# Challenge
# of Change

Realize who you are ~
to become what you must.
Though the newness
may seem  strange.

Meet today with courage,
tomorrow with trust,
As you welcome
the challenge of change.

Something new may be meeting a need,
And needs change as one grows.
Many a change transforms a seed
Before it becomes a rose.

But if the seed  were to shrink from the sun
And cling instead to the earth,
The bud would never be begun,
Nor could the rose find birth.

Don't cling with fear to the tried and true,
Remember, it too, once was new.
Greet life eagerly, ever knowing ~
Ever changing means ever growing.

© Pat Sampson

# Bernie Siegel, M.D.

**Dr. Bernie Siegel,** (Bernie, as he prefers), founded Exceptional Cancer Patients (ECaP) in 1978. He is one of the world's foremost physicians, authors, motivational speakers and advocates for individuals facing the challenges of all chronic illnesses. His many articles, best-selling books, tapes and videos serve as a testimony to his loving commitment for those who wish to take an active role in their own healing process. He and his wife Bobbie have introduced the concept of individual and group therapy based on "carefrontation," a loving, safe, therapeutic confrontation enabling everyone to understand his or her healing potential. Motivational, inspirational and down-to-earth, Bernie's approach is one of compassion, caring and love coupled with a wonderful sense of humor. His message of hope and love is extended to all. His runaway best sellers include: *Love, Medicine & Miracles; Peace, Love & Healing; How to Live Between Office Visits* and *Prescriptions for Living.*

The Mind-Body Wellness Center is the on-line home of
ECaP - Exceptional Cancer Patients,
an organization founded by Bernie Siegel, MD,
in 1978 and dedicated to providing tools,
information and resources
for individuals challenged by chronic illnesses.
*http://www.mind-body.org/Bernie.HTM*

T he first thought that enters my mind when I consider the future of healing is that it will be returned to where it really comes from. We are the healers. The wisdom is within us, and not in what is prescribed for us.

Stop and ask yourself how does a wound heal? What wisdom is within us that unites us and makes us whole again. How does a single cell know how to create a human being and put all the parts where they belong? What makes the edges of a wound grow together?

I don't know but I rely on my body's ability to do it every day. There is incredible wisdom, desire to heal and will to live in every cell. I am always amazed at what nature teaches us in simple ways and clear cut lessons.

The *Bible* does tell us to look to the plants and animals and they will teach us. Barbed wire is nailed to a tree and the tree is not irritated by the wire but grows around it and takes it in. A chain link fence is put up but the tree refuses to be limited and grows through the chain links. A road is paved and a few weeks later the pavement cracks and out pops a skunk cabbage plant. How did they know how to do that?

What wisdom is within the seed to tell it which way to grow and to not accept the resistance to its growth. How many of us defy the odds and fight to survive with the same desire as that skunk cabbage seed. Nature is my teacher and therapist.

I have started a new religion called, *Undo.* Hopefully, once it is established it will undo the harm done by beliefs of the past. The significant symbols of my religion are a penny, ice, band aid and the number "10."

A penny tells us, *In God We Trust* and *Liberty*, important messages for healing and surviving. Ice, by defying the laws of physics, teaches us what is possible when one is a creator. Every liquid when frozen become more dense and sinks except water.

Why? Because if life is going to survive we need to keep the ice on top or all the life in the seas would be destroyed. Now who thought of that ahead of time?

My favorite symbol is the band aid. When God gave us the ability to form scabs and heal our wounds, so that we would not bleed to death or die of an infection each time we were injured, God didn't know that people have bad habits. We pick on the scabs and interfere with the process of healing. Well God came up with a solution called a band aid to cover the wound and hide it. Lo and behold the wound heals faster without interference from people.

The number "10" also relates to our wholeness and healing of relationships. Think of how many times the number ten, or multiples of ten, appear to be significant. Commandments, attractive women, perfect test scores, enough good people to save a city or hold a Jewish service, fingers and toes, the sum of 1+2+3+4=10 and the computer system relying on the 1 and the 0.

What does it have to tell us? The numbers which add up to ten speak of The One and our relationships with The One. When we relate ourselves, each other and the family of man to The One we add up to ten and will heal the planet by becoming one family. Please remember we are all the same color inside and truly of one family derived from The One who parents us all. The One is derived from the undifferentiated potential which is really not nothing but more like a blank canvas with the potential to create and from it we all come. That is why evolution has left us with ten fingers and toes rather than eliminate unnecessary toes and add fingers. Ten is a reminder of our wholeness and ability to heal.

To heal I might add is different than to cure. We are all mortal and cannot cure every affliction but we can always heal. Some of the greatest healers I know have physical disabilities that cannot be cured. I cannot replace an amputated body part but the person can be whole and heal. We need to remember that healing transcends the body but I also know that when one transcends the physical limitations, true healing occurs and with true healing some amazing cures are produced as by products.

A healed life provides live messages and a healing environment for the body. The words of a woman who had a mastectomy enter my mind, "Do we perhaps shed things as we go through life that other features may be enhanced?" The answer is *yes*. We prune the tree and it remains healthy.

The future of healing lies with each one of us. Heal your life by giving it meaning and no physical affliction will ever be able to control your life. Helen Keller is an example and if you haven't read her autobiography, do so.

Last but not least remember that death can be the ultimate and final healing. When you grow tired of your body because it cannot serve you any longer then do what my 97 year old, quadriplegic, father-in-law did. He left his body and just fell up. Of course the more healing you do in this life time, the easier the next one will seem.

# The Most Important Thing I Know About Love

I know that love is the most powerful, indestructible force and substance in the universe. For this reason, I call love the brick from which all of life is constructed. I also believe laughter is the mortar which holds the bricks together. If love weren't a part of the creative, intelligent energy that many refer to as God, we would never have developed our ability to heal.

> *Love heals. Love is the belief in the sanctity of all things; compassion for ourselves; forgiveness for the parts of ourselves that are learning. It is about softening and opening ourselves to broaden experience and disengaging from easy judgmentalism.*

Why I call love a potent force or substance is because of what it can do when expressed. It is no accident we have sayings such as, "love is blind," "kill 'em with kindness" and "love thine enemies." Enemies are obliterated by love and faults are not seen in loved ones. If the world were filled with lovers, there would be no wars or conflicts. In Doestoyevsky's *The Grand Inquisitor*, the prisoner is set free when in response to the cruelty of the Inquisitor who is going to burn and crucify him the next morning, he gives him a kiss on his aged lips. Read Corinthians I:13 for further details about love's qualities.

Since love is also immortal, I want something that won't wear out supporting it. In a Hindu story, a boy with his parents' consent, volunteers to give his life to save others. He obtains their consent by telling them, "Consider this sooner or later, my body will perish at any rate, but if it perishes without love which the wise declare is the only thing of permanence, of what use will it have been?" We are here to serve, not be served, and each of us needs to express our love in our unique way.

Two of my favorite writers share the same thoughts. Thornton Wilder wrote in *The Bridge of San Luis Rey*, "And we ourselves shall be loved for awhile and forgotten but the love will have been enough. All those impulses of love return to the love that made them. Even memory is not necessary for love. There is a land of the living and a land of the dead and the bridge is love. The only survival the only meaning."

William Saroyan in *The Human Comedy* wrote, "The best part of a good man stays. It stays forever, for love is immortal and makes all things immortal, but hate dies every minute."

So the most important thing I know about love is that it heals all wounds, eliminates all enemies, heals the giver and the receiver, protects us from illness, cures afflictions and changes those who are loved.

My role models, as I struggle to be a lover, are Lassie and Don Quixote. I have seen what their love can do and when in difficult situations, I ask myself what they would do. Feel free to use your own role models and find your own way to serve and discover your immortality.

---

*Work like you don't need the money,*
*Dance like no one is watching*
*And love like you've never been hurt*

**- Lao Tzu**

---

# Thoughts on Health

**Proverbs 17:22**
A merry heart doeth good like a medicine.

**Buddha**
The secret for health for both body and mind is to live in
the present moment wisely and earnestly.

**Wayne Dyer**
When you begin to heal the inner you, you alter your immune system.

**Naomi Judd**
Every day I still get down on my knees to thank God I'm back on my feet!

**Seneca**
It is part of the cure to wish to be cured.

**Anonymous**
Ulcers aren't the result of what you eat. You get ulcers from what's eating you.

**Will Kommen**
If you look like your passport photo, you're too ill to travel.

**Cher**
Fitness: If it came in a bottle, everybody would have a good body.

**Earl of Derby**
Those who do not find time to exercise will have to find time for illness.

**Ronald J. Pion**
You are in charge of your state of being. You have learned to be exactly the
way you are and you have the remarkable human capability to learn to
be another way. Choosing ways of thinking, feeling, and doing which
contribute to your health pleasures rather than your health
problems is the nitty-gritty of being well.

**Deepak Chopra**
You can reverse your biological age by changing your perceptions.

**Norman Cousins**
The human body experiences a powerful gravitational pull in the direction of
hope. That is why the patient's hopes are the physician's secret weapon.
They are the hidden ingredients in any prescription.

**George Bernard Shaw**
Use your health, even to the point of wearing it out. That is what it is for. Spend
all you have before you die; and do not outlive yourself.

**Abraham Lincoln**
In the end, it's not the years in your life that count; it's the life in your years.

**John Andrew Holmes**
There is no exercise better for the heart than reaching down
and lifting people up.

# Ben Mull

**Ben Mull** is a Baby Boomer out to redefine "Senior Citizen" through healthy living and energetic service. Young at heart, enthusiastic about life, questing and hopeful, to many who are younger, he is inspirational. Ben grew up and makes his home outside Washington, DC. His community commitment includes two years with the U.S. Army and 40 years as a volunteer emergency medical technician. He considers educating others about healthy lifestyles a part of his community service. In this new career he has helped scores of people enjoy improved well being - one he finds intensely rewarding.

Radiant health tops almost everyone's list as the basis for the good life. We feel as if anything is possible when we glow with strength and well-being.

For decades, conventional medical wisdom decreed that the food we eat can supply all nutrients needed for good health. That viewpoint has now dramatically changed. A recent scientific review in the *Journal of the American Medical Association* finds that a "large portion" of the general population doesn't get enough vitamins from our daily diet to prevent chronic degenerative diseases. JAMA cautions that vitamin deficiency is associated with increased risk of coronary heart disease, cancer, and osteoporosis. The research concludes that *"it appears prudent for all adults to take vitamin supplements."*

I discovered the truth of that statement six years ago when I began experiencing the same health conditions that preceded my father's chronic heart disease. I explored every lead in collecting information to help myself, eventually adopting a wellness program offered by a cutting-edge company specializing in nutritional supplements. The products meet strict criteria that anyone should apply when purchasing supplements:

- formulas based on sound research
- a pharmaceutical-grade production process
- stringent quality-control to guarantee potency

The lifestyle changes I adopted have transformed my health to the point that I've gone into business to share the information with as many people as possible. Contact me for a free consultation about a wellness program to meet your needs.

Website: *www.unitoday.net/ben mull*
Phone: (301) 490-1644
Ben Mull, P.O. Box 608, Burtonsville, MD 20866

# What Is Youth

Youth is not a time of life; it is a state of mind. It is not a matter of ripe cheeks, red lips, supple knees; it is a temper of the will, a quality of the imagination, a vigor of the emotions; it is a freshness of the deep springs of life. Youth means a temperamental predominance of courage over timidity, of the appetite of adventure over the love of ease. This often exists in a man of fifty more than a boy of twenty. Nobody grows old merely living a number of years; people grow old only by deserting their ideals. Years may wrinkle the skin, but to give up enthusiasm wrinkles the soul.

Worry, doubt, self-doubt, fear and despair, these are the long, long years that bow the head and turn the growing spirit back to dust. Whether seventy or seventeen there is in every being's heart the love of wonder, the sweet amazement of the stars and starlight things and thoughts, the undaunted challenge of events, the unfailing childlike appetite for what is next, and the joy of the game of life.

You are as young as your faith, as old as your doubt; as young as your self-confidence, as old as your fear; as young as your hope, as old as your despair.

In the central place of your heart there is a sensitive person. So long as it receives messages of beauty, hope, cheer, grandeur, courage and power from the earth, from men and from the infinite, are you young.

~ Anonymous

# JUNE L. THOMPSON

**June L. Thompson**, a mother and very proud grandmother, spends her time giving back to the community. She is a great friend who seeks to find out more about people and their hopes and dreams. Deeply committed to her work with families in hospice care, her greatest joy comes from working as a volunteer. **Amera**, her home-based health and beauty business, allows her to share knowledge on how to enhance natural beauty and health by using the right products to achieve optimum results. June leads a fulfilling life based on service in both her personal and business endeavors; and is recognized by friends and community alike for her many contributions.

Taking time to give of one's self is so rewarding. Volunteer work blesses the giver at least as much as those to whom we give. Most of us are so blessed in this society, that the impulse to help others should come without a moment's hesitation. It matters less what we have to give, than that we make the effort to share our hearts and skills. In the end it is ourselves we are giving and in the act of sharing love and talents we may not even have been aware of, we often discover in the eyes and faces of those we tend to just who we ourselves truly are.

The turning point in my own development came about as I dealt with care giving centered on my own parents' illnesses. In caring for them, I learned what giving is all about. An inner awareness began to surface on how giving back to others would help me to heal my own pain and loss. Hospice Caring came into my life at just that point. Participating in hospice work is such a blessing. In the process of offering support to others and helping them with their needs - either in their homes or in the hospital, we get to feel needed. Hospice caring is a non-profit group that provides support and comfort to people with terminal illnesses and to their families.

As a volunteer, you undergo training on how to comfort people who may be unable to effectively communicate their needs. One would believe working with the terminally ill would be depressing, but the truth is quite the opposite. Those in the final stages of life often have much to teach us about living. My work with Hospice has given me a new perspective on life, one I am deeply grateful for and recommend to others.

**Contact June:**
*jlt4amera@rcn.com*
**or (301) 963-1091**

# Thoughts on Listening

**Walter Anderson**
Good listeners, like precious gems, are to be treasured.

**Calvin Coolidge**
No one ever listened themselves out of a job.

**Dalai Lama**
Remember that silence is sometimes the best answer.

**Turkish Proverb**
If speaking is silver, then listening is gold.

**Peter deLisser**
Listening to another individual is like Michelangelo's description of sculpting.
I chip away at a block of stone to reveal the work of art already inside.

**Leo Buscaglia**
Too often we underestimate the power of a touch, a smile, a kind word,
a listening ear, an honest compliment, or the smallest act of caring,
all of which have the potential to turn a life around.

**Anonymous**
When making personal decisions, listen to what your head says; then listen to
what your heart says. If they differ, follow your heart! When you listen to your
heart, you listen to that part of you most interested in your well-being.

**Dr. E. H. Mayo**
One friend, one person who is truly understanding, who takes the trouble to listen
to us as we consider a problem, can change our whole outlook on the world.

**Karl Menninger**
Listening is a magnetic and strange thing a creative force. The friends who
listen to us are the ones we move toward. When we are listened to,
it creates us, makes us unfold and expand.

**Anonymous**
Opportunities are often missed because we are broadcasting
when we should be listening.

**e.e. cummings**
We do not believe in ourselves until someone reveals that deep inside us is
something valuable, worth listening to, worthy of our trust, sacred to our touch.
Once we believe in ourselves we can risk curiosity, wonder, spontaneous
delight or any experience that reveals the human spirit.

**Sarah Ban Breathnach**
Greet everyone you meet with a warm smile. No matter how busy you are,
don't rush encounters with coworkers, family, and friends. Speak softly. Listen
attentively. Act as if every conversation you have is the most important thing
on your mind today. Look your children and your partner in the eyes when
they talk to you. Stroke the cat, caress the dog, lavish love on every living
being you meet. See how different you feel at the end of the day.

# ESPERANZA REY

**Esperanza Rey** is a workshop leader, transpersonal therapist, teacher, translator, interpreter and systems engineer. She is helping to pave the way for a new awareness. In the last 20 years she has traveled extensively learning a variety of disciplines and methodologies taught by great master teachers. She has taught in the USA and Europe. Esperanza worked with at risk teenagers, prisoners and the homeless to help them achieve greater stability and balance. Esperanza has considerable experience in the area of Past Life Regression, Quantum Healing, Energy Body Expansion, Grid/Vortex Clearing and Activation and Cranial-Sacral Therapy. She is currently writing her book *Experiences With Angels*

Quantum Physics shows that all particles are interconnected with consciousness. Your body is a psychotronic machine, meaning that your thoughts and belief patterns directly affect your physical body. Your thoughts, words and actions carry your intent, which also affect the perception and response of others. Understanding these reactions can mean the success or failure of your goals.

You can recondition your mental/emotional state of being. Experience the healing with ancient yogic exercises and meditation. Restore the natural production of hormones that regenerate your body, mind and spirit.

- Purify and rejuvenate yourself
- Expand your awareness
- Call back your power
- Realize your full potential

Learn to remove what is blocking your energy and bring yourself to optimal health. Expand your consciousness and develop your intuitive and healing abilities. Connect to the deepest aspects of your higher consciousness. Embrace love and peace within the Godhead. Address the spiritual nature of your true self and purpose. Find your inner-sanctuary. Regain and maintain your balance. Free yourself of limitations and fears. Transmute and release negativity from yourself, others and the environment.

**Inner Awareness Center – "The Journey Inside Self"**
**Esperanza Rey – Transpersonal Therapist and**
**Workshop Leader**
**(703) 569-4912**
*Esp.Rey@verizon.net*

# LISTEN TO YOUR THOUGHTS

*"You are today where your thoughts have brought you.*
*You will be tomorrow where your thoughts take you."*
~ James Lane Allen

You are the builder ~ the maker and shaper of your own destiny. Your thoughts direct the course of your life so listen to them. Become aware of the kind of dialogue you keep feeding yourself. In this way, you get a sense of the limitations you might be putting on yourself and your world. If you don't like the direction they are taking you, change them in a positive way to tap the confidence and resilience you already possess.

You can use your thoughts correctly or let them use you. Daily, hourly, by the second, you choose your thoughts. Then, one day, everything upon which you focus comes rushing to you, as if your thoughts were a magnet. So fast does it come that you have no time to change positions or get out of the way. This represents an unchanging universal law: you attract to yourself those things upon which you dwell.

The law works whether you acknowledge it or not. You consistently bring scenes to life that which you mentally rehearse. In the past, you may have unwittingly given your attention to conditions of deficiency; now, give your attention to conditions of prosperity to empower your higher mind with the mental and spiritual energy to make your dreams come true.

Change the way you think and you change the way you see life. Change the way you see life and life is new. Say that you are well and all is well with you! Think on the good things and watch as life lovingly rewards you with the good things! Knowing that all things are possible gives you access to a power that can be tapped ~ and then used ~ by those who learn to become attuned to its presence.

The obvious improvement in health and well being, the dynamic sense of purpose, the ability to enjoy all the marvels that life has to offer, inspires the self-confidence and self-esteem to walk out of the shadows of your fears and into the positive, bright aspects of your own inner light.

# ADARA L. WALTON, N.D.

**Reverend Adara L. Walton, N.D.** is an ordained minister, Doctor of Naturopathy, Bio-Energy Kinesiologist, certified Basic Attractor Field Technique Practitioner, Heart & Soul Practitioner and Reiki/Amanohuna Teacher and practitioner. She has been studying and working with the human energy fields for the past 16 years, using Aromatherapy, Homeopathy, color, sound and light in her dynamic healing practice called **HeartBridge Wellness, L.L.C. (formerly Spiritual Education Attunement for Living - S.E.A.L.).** Educating the client in self-healing is the foundation of her healing practice as the body unlocks its truth. Rev. Walton's affordable sessions are open to adults and children of all ages.

Rev. Walton conducts sessions that involve releasing stress from all levels of the body, balancing the mental, emotional, physical and spiritual levels through the wisdom of the body called "muscle testing." Having masterships in different forms of Reiki and Amanohuna allows the gentle use of the "laying on of hands" while her knowledge of frequencies (sound/color/light) repair and balance the meridian and chakra systems.

The Attractor Field Technique (AFT) allows the client to gently "tap" out the disorder, dis-ease/stress from the body and to release addictions and phobias like smoking and fear of public speaking. Financial, career/work and relationship issues can be addressed through energetic balancing while Aromatherapy and Homeopathy can be used to address physical and emotional issues to energize or relax the body. Nutritional balances and counseling offer education on diet and weight issues, supplements, cleansing and fasting. Special sessions are conducted for those who are deaf, hospitalized or incapacitated. Generally, sessions are 60 minutes or longer, if needed, or upon request during evening hours and/or Saturday. Avail yourself of Rev. Walton's natural and empowering self-healing sessions by contacting her today.

**Call Rev. Walton and Get in Touch with Yourself**
**By Appointment only**
**410-799-8066**
**Ellicott City, MD**

# THINK ON THE GOOD THINGS

"Whatsoever things are good ~ whatsoever things are true ~ whatsoever things are pure ~ think on these things."
~ Philippians 4:8

A Great Teacher said that more than 2,000 years ago and its message is still the same. *"Think on the good things."* This kind of thinking is powerful medicine; it not only prevents negativity, it cures it. Focusing attention on positives produces more positives, especially when the chips are down.

It is natural to be of good cheer when the sun is shining but when you cling to a sunny disposition while thoroughly being drenched by a passing storm, you are on your way to freedom ~ freedom from limitation ~ freedom from circumstance.

There is a classic tale that illustrates this graphically. It is a story of two stonecutters, both laboring in the hot sun for meager wages. A passerby who stopped to inquire the nature of their tasks was answered rudely by one: *"What does it look like I'm dong? I'm cutting stone."* The other stonecutter replied: *"I'm building a temple."* The second stonecutter, by thinking on the good things, was easing his task and gaining the inner satisfaction that gave meaning to his life.

Seeing the good does not mean whitewashing those things that need change. It means feeling good enough about yourself to make choices that produce the greatest good. Will you make this day happy for yourself and others? Or will you choose doom and gloom? Tip the scale to the bright side with the spirit of hope. If you think life is beautiful, you will see beauty where others see nothing.

Your thoughts are guaranteed to attract whatever is heartfelt. The best thing you can do for your health is to believe that your body is a magnet attracting vibrations of strength, vigor and vitality. The best thing you can do for your finances is to picture yourself ever in touch with the source of all supply. The best thing you can do for your relationships is to acknowledge and appreciate the people in your life. Do your best in every situation and then leave it with the words: *"I can hardly wait to see what good will come of this."*

# Mark Bottinick

**Mark Bottinick** is a licensed, certified clinical social worker. He provides therapy and coaching to adults, children, and adolescents both in his Maryland office and over the phone. Mark also conducts workshops for clinical professionals and the public. His clients have ranged from high-level professionals and public figures to individuals with severe mental illness and addictions. *"My approach is holistic. I combine traditional therapy with self-help techniques that are on the cutting-edge."*

For more information, visit *www.reallygoodtherapist. com*, e-mail him at *mbottinick@hotmail.com* or call 301-593-7494.

# When Positive
# Seems Impossible

At times, a positive attitude can seem utterly out of reach. When clients come to my therapy practice with "negative" emotions that seem to them insurmountable, my fundamental task is to help them regain hope. Although I'm an optimist by nature, my optimism has grown much stronger over the last several years as I've witnessed extraordinary healing. Often, the transformations occurred rapidly and almost effortlessly, shattering the conventional wisdom about the possibilities for personal change.

There is a quiet revolution underway. Around the world, therapists and the general public are discovering that it is possible to quickly alleviate troubling emotions, beliefs, and even some physical symptoms with new, highly unconventional techniques. Perhaps because these tools are so unconventional, they have not yet gained mainstream awareness. Because I'm committed to spreading the word, I'll share with you details on my favorite tool for creating change.

Emotional Freedom Technique (EFT) is a surprisingly simple procedure based on the principals of acupuncture (but without the needles!). The technique empowers my clients to gain more control over their feelings and thoughts, and consequently, their behavior, than they ever imagined possible. I help my clients to make the best use of the tool during our sessions and they gain a lifelong skill that they can practice on their own.

The theory underlying Emotional Freedom Technique maintains that there is an energetic nature to the human body and to one's thoughts and feelings. Flows of energy in the body rise to the surface of the skin at "acupuncture points."

You can affect your body's energy system and in turn, your thoughts and feelings, by focusing awareness on the problematic feeling or belief while tapping with fingers on particular acupuncture points. The feeling or belief begins to lessen in intensity until it is significantly or completely resolved. Results are often very long lasting.

Here's a typical example: A client complains that after a traumatic car accident, he has become a very nervous driver, unable to travel on highways, which is having a negative impact on his work and home life. We spend some time talking about his experience and the specific thoughts and fears that come to him while driving, making a list of issues to target. One issue on the list might be a recurring fearful thought that "a truck might hit me." I direct my client to imagine driving on the highway and allow the fear of "a truck might hit me" to arise, and then concentrate on this feeling while tapping the EFT acupuncture points. After several minutes, my client reports that he is no longer able to access this fearful thought. We continue to address the rest of the related issues on the list including the upsetting memories of the accident. Ultimately, he is able to recall the accident without an emotional reaction and is able to drive again without undue fear. We move on to other issues and the problems with driving do not reoccur.

Can it really be this easy? Years ago, I thought the notion of tapping away problems sounded preposterous. I couldn't foresee that I would one day call upon EFT to help me cope with profound loss in my own life. Now, having taught EFT to hundreds of clients, friends and other therapists, I have had the rich reward of seeing people transform themselves. Psychiatrist Alice Lee-Bloem reported back to me, "I have proven to myself again and again that if I apply the simple methods, amazing healing can occur at a tremendous pace."

EFT isn't magic. It won't make all your problems disappear unless you're already living a very blessed life. But in my experience, when applied by a skilled practitioner, Emotional Freedom Technique vastly accelerates the pace of change and sometimes enables change that would be very difficult with traditional methods of therapy.

Viewed most simply, EFT allows us to address challenges with greater speed and efficiency. Yet on a deeper level, once we bear witness to the power of our own life energy, we are forever expanded. The experience calls us to question our self-imposed limits, to push against our boundaries, to see new possibilities for ourselves and for the world.

# STEVEN M. ROTTER, M.D.

**Dr. Steven M. Rotter,** a native Washingtonian, completed two years of residency in general surgery, followed by a three-year dermatology residency at Johns Hopkins Hospital, during which he became the Chief Resident in Dermatology. Dr. Rotter was then awarded prestigious fellowship training in Mohs Micrographic and Dermatologic Surgery at the University of Pennsylvania.

He is drawn to his specialty much like an architect or builder enjoys creating harmony and balance in a structure. "I can see my work take shape" says Dr. Rotter, "and enjoy the satisfaction of my patients being happy with the results."

His comprehensive background has given Dr. Rotter a complete understanding of skin processes. He remains committed to continuing his education in the latest, most effective methods for restoring a youthful appearance, refining facial features, and concealing skin imperfections. This includes obtaining the most up-to-date laser equipment to offer patients the widest range of treatments possible.

Conditions treated include wrinkled and sagging skin, scars, tattoos, brown spots, blemishes, spider and varicose veins, birthmarks, roacea, skin cancer, and unwanted hair. Dr. Rotter and his team also recommend quality skin rejuvenation and maintenance products.

Extensive experience and training at prestigious institutions are the professional qualifications that set Dr. Steven Rotter apart from his peers. Years of personal dedication to excellence and individualized attention are what set him apart with his patients.

**The Center for Cosmetic, Laser & Dermatologic Surgery**
**7700 Leesburg Pike, Suite 423**
**Falls Church, Virginia**
**(703) 442-0300** *www.wedoskin.com*

If the body is the temple of the soul, the skin is its encasement, the first thing we see as we greet each other. When tended with care, skin reflects vibrant good health and sends out a positive message to those around us. While "looks aren't everything," the way we present ourselves has an undeniable influence on how others perceive us.

Looking our best must bear the same relationship to being as any other human attribute: wholeness, the need to involve the totality of the person, starting with the very way we perceive our potential. Cosmetic enhancement is no longer limited to the rich and famous. Growing demand and advances in technology have made the quest for eternal beauty affordable for almost everyone.

Cosmetic enhancement can be a boon to your confidence and change the image you project to the world. When you've become so self-conscious that thinking about your perceived defect is making your life less enjoyable, cosmetic surgery may offer you a way to open up to life again.

Becoming your best begins with trust. "The key is choosing a surgeon with your best interest in mind," according to Dr. Rotter. Achieving the best results begins long before the day of your procedure. Every patient deserves a surgeon who takes every step necessary to ensure the greatest satisfaction possible.

- One-on-one consultations that provide all the information necessary for an informed decision.

- Careful listening to understand a patient's motivation. "We try to emphasize that each procedure brings about physical changes, but it's up to you to decide how that's going to change your life," explains Dr. Rotter.

- Recommending procedures that will have the most positive effect for the smallest impact. "My philosophy is that we don't do anything that the person doesn't need to have done," says Dr. Rotter. "If a full face lift would make only a small improvement on a minimal defect, I will recommend another procedure."

Cosmetic surgery cannot fulfill the promise of eternal beauty, but in well-trained, caring hands, it can help restore you to feeling and looking your best. This creates a sense of well-being that will be contagious, so that you will make others feel as good as you do.

# Mark N. Levy, DPM., P.A.

**Dr. Levy** is a Diplomate of the American Board of Podiatric Surgery and a Fellow of the American College of Foot and Ankle Surgery. He graduated Cum Laude from the New York College of Podiatric Medicine and has been in practice in Rockville, Maryland for 23 years. One of the most highly respected podiatrists on the East Coast, Dr. Levy specializes in biomechanics and the etiology of foot pathology. A favorite of athletes, runners and physical fitness advocates, Dr. Levy is also a devoted husband and father.

Until they start hurting – most of us don't give much thought to our feet, yet without them we couldn't stand, walk, run, dance or do a host of other wonderful things. If you will pardon the joke, feet come in very "handy." They are the root of physical fitness and if properly attended, allow you to walk through life with a smile instead of a grimace. But too many of us treat our feet with very little respect. As a result, I see patients with a lot of heel spurs and bunions and unnecessary pain.

Like the whole of the human body, feet are miraculous mechanisms. The human foot is an amazing and complex structure. Each foot has 26 major bones, plus muscles, nerves, ligaments, and blood vessels. Amazingly, the bones in your feet make up about one-fourth of all the bones in the body. Our feet – when they are well cared for – give us balance and mobility.

Whether you are an athlete, a marathon runner, a teacher, baker, candle-stick-maker, mother, father – whatever you do in this life – your feet are the support structures on which your physical well being rests. Treat them well and they will move you effortlessly through your life. Putting your best foot forward enables you to put your best self forward and to walk through life with positive, happy steps.

**For consultation contact Dr. Levy:**
**1201 Seven Locks Road, Suite 202**
**Rockville, Maryland (301) 762-4636**

# DR. ALISON F. HENDERSON

**Dr. Alison Henderson** recognized early on the body's innate ability to guide us toward well-being if we pay it proper attention. She experienced the mind/body/spirit training that accompanies becoming a National Taekwondo Champion and has seen first hand as a Holistic Chiropractor and Physiotherapist the body's ability to heal itself given proper care and the willingness of the human spirit inhabiting it. Dr. Henderson is also a certified reflexologist and colon hydro therapist. Founder of the non-profit New Life Community Wellness Center, whose mission is to provide health care to everyone, regardless of their ability to pay, Dr. Henderson believes in the individuality of healing, and that everyone has a right to medical care regardless of their financial or professional status.

Dr. Henderson takes a mind/body/spirit approach to better health. She has a strong conviction that preventive maintenance is the key to health, and chiropractic care, along with healthy eating and exercise, should be an integral part of fitness and disease prevention for most people. Her gentle, soft touch, painless technique places the bones in the neck and back into their proper position and eases muscles back to health through massage and physical therapy.

Because wellness is much more than bone and muscle alignment, Dr. Henderson also advises clients on nutrition, stress and weight reduction, exercise, and proper posture. Emotional balance is encouraged through meditation and prayer.

She has developed a strong belief confirmed by daily experience, that pain and other physical symptoms should not be dismissed and masked, because they steer us toward finding the underlying cause of our problems. She likens ignoring uncomfortable symptoms to turning off a fire alarm and continuing on with daily activities -disabling the alarm doesn't put out the fire!

Her holistic approach has assisted clients with arthritis; carpal tunnel; disc problems; headaches; pain in the back, knee, elbow, shoulder, and neck; recovery from accidents and sports injuries; and sciatica. Nutritional and herbal advice also helps people with more serious challenges like AIDS, cancer and hepatitis.

**Reach Dr. Henderson at:**
**202-293-2225 or 202-544-4478**
**Email:** *chiroal@aol.com*
**Website:** *www.newlifewellness.meta-ehealth.com*

# SAL T. HAKIM, Ph.D

**Sal Hakim** is a strong advocate of clean air for better health. He has devoted many years in medical research during his tenure as a professor and medical researcher in prestigious medical schools to understanding the impact of the environment on the lungs and the heart. His many published articles have appeared and been reviewed in scientific and medical journals. As a scientist knowledgeable in the impact of the environment on our health, he is dedicated to educating the public on the importance of healthy indoor air quality and how to avoid exposure to air pollution.

Everyone knows that to keep up with our fast-paced lives, the name of the game is energy and sound physical condition. Breathing cleaner air is associated with better health, better mind, and longer life span. You need to become aware of the air you breathe in your home and office environment. Did you know, for instance, that the EPA has announced that indoor air quality is a major public health concern? That outdoor air is, in fact, healthier than indoor air? The reasons are clear. We seal our homes and offices from the outside world as much as possible to reduce heating and cooling costs. This practice allows chemicals and levels of pollution to build up rapidly. This is where the term "sick home syndrome"(SHS) or "sick building syndrome"(SBS) comes from.

Personally, I derive much fulfillment in knowing that the knowledge to which I have been privy throughout my career, enables me to keep the public informed of the best scientific information and products available to combat this very real threat to our health and well being. For the person concerned with an optimum health environment for yourself and your family, as well as for allergy and asthma suffers and chemical sensitivity, you will find a myriad of doctor recommended products and scientific information ~ together in one place. Come visit. You'll be glad you did.

**Allergy & Asthma Store**
**Gaithersburg, MD**
**(301) 527 – 8711,** *www.forallergy.com*

# Thoughts on Nature

**Charles Panati**
We are the environment.

**Albert Einstein**
The joy of looking and comprehending is nature's most beautiful gift.

**Theodore Roosevelt**
To waste, to destroy our natural resources, to skin and exhaust the land
instead of using it so as to increase its usefulness, will result in undermining
in the days of our children the very prosperity which we ought by right
to hand down to them amplified and developed.

**Chief Seattle**
Humankind has not woven the web of life. We are but one thread within it.
Whatever we do to the web, we do to ourselves. All things
are bound together . . .all things connect.

**Elizabeth Goudge**
Nothing living should ever be treated with contempt. Whatever it is that lives,
a man, a tree, or a bird, should be touched gently, because the time is short.
Civilization is another word for respect for life.

**Robert Green Ingersoll**
In nature there are neither rewards nor punishments—there are consequences.

**Selwynn Champion**
Cutting down a weed is not so good as uprooting it.

**James Carswell**
Whenever man comes up with a better mousetrap, nature immediately
comes up with a better mouse.

**William Law**
All that is sweet, delightful, and amiable in this world, in the serenity of the air,
the fineness of seasons, the joy of light, the melody of sounds, the beauty of
colors, the fragrancy of smells, the splendor of our precious stones, is nothing
else but Heaven breaking through the veil of this world, manifesting itself in
such a degree and darting forth in such variety so much of its own nature.

**Mahatma Gandhi**
The greatness of a nation and its moral progress can be judged
by the way animals are treated.

**George Washington Carver**
I love to think of nature as an unlimited broadcasting station, through
Which God speaks to us every hour, If we will only tune in.

**Parks Cousin**
How things look on the outside of us depends on how things are on the inside
of us. Stay close to the heart of nature and forget this troubled world.
Remember, there is nothing wrong with nature; the trouble is in ourselves.

**Goethe**
The world is so empty if one thinks only of mountains, rivers and cities; but to
know someone who thinks and feels with us, and though distant, is close
to us in spirit—this makes the earth for us an inhabited garden.

# ANNA MOORE CARROLL

**Anna Carroll**, Holistic Advisor, was diagnosed with a terminal illness some years ago caused by second-hand tobacco smoke in the workplace. It turned out to be one of those gifts that sometimes come through difficult circumstances as it led her into the study of her illness and its causes. In the process of looking for answers, she reconnected to her Native American heritage and to childhood memories of growing up in Jackson County, Alabama in the southern Appalachian Mountains, and listening to her grandmother and aunts talk about different herbs they used to treat illnesses in their families. "I remembered walking with them through nature as they described the healing properties of various plants we saw along the way," she recalls.

In the time since her illness, on the journey of searching for answers, Anna Carroll has continued to study and learn all she can about the life enhancing gifts with which we are blessed by the plant kingdom. Today, her life's purpose is found in working with one of nature's most powerful, holistic health solutions ~ therapeutic-grade essential oils. "Pursuing it," she says, " I still walk in spirit with my grandmother and aunts, continuing the family and cultural tradition of sharing the healing wisdom that has not only survived but has become revered throughout the centuries for their restorative properties for body, mind and spirit."

Contact Anna at carroll.A@erols.com
P.O. Box 8152, Alexandria, Va. 22306

# Native American Culture

*"The physical world is real. The Spiritual world is real. They are two aspects of one reality. There are separate laws which govern each. Breaking of a spiritual principle will affect the physical world and visa versa. A balanced life is one that honors both"*

— Ancient Native American Wisdom

I am proud of my Cherokee heritage. Although native culture is as diverse as the many wide-ranging tribal peoples who were once the sole inhabitants of the North American continent, there are some basic cultural imperatives common to them all, most especially a reverence for and deep loving connectedness to Mother Earth and a belief in the connectedness of Spirit and all beings.

My ancestors held a close connection to the earth. They recognized and respected their fellow beings on this planet – be they animals, trees, rocks, and plants – and as a result they also understood the interrelationship of all life forms. The grandmothers and aunts did not memorize facts from books. The things they taught were part of a long oral tradition of knowledge passed from generation to generation – and learned anew from generation to generation.

Native healers "listen" to the spirit of the plants and herbs they use. And they never forget to express their gratitude. Native American cultures view plants, animals and the earth itself as having their own consciousness. Traditional healers gave thanks and left an offering when they took from a living plant to use its leaves or roots. This understanding of the importance of gratitude is connected to the spiritual understanding of the oneness of all things. As we know from so many of our tribal ceremonies, putting our mind and our bodies in harmony with the universal order begins with assuming personal responsibility, and by staying in harmony with others. I am grateful for the gift of my heritage, grateful for who I am and glad to share what I have learned in hopes of doing my small part in making the world a better and healthier place.

## Essential Oils for Pleasure and Well Being

Mother Nature's garden provides gifts of flowers, trees, and herbs to enhance our lives in a powerful way. My ancestors, the Cherokee Indians, used the healing power of plant extracts to energize, relax, stimulate and create overall wellness. Today we are enjoying a renaissance as people are re-discovering the wisdom passed down through the ages of the gentleness and effectiveness of using botanical oils for well being of mind, body, and spirit. With the use of essential oils, many of these benefits can now be extended into our daily lives.

### *The A List of Essential Oils:*

*Basil, Bergamot, Seed, Cedarwood, Chamomile, Clary Sage, Clove, Cypress, Eucalyptus, Fir, Frankincense, Geranium, Helichrysum, Jasmine, Lavender, Lemon, Marjoram, Melaleuca, Myrrh, Myrtle, Nutmeg, Orange, Peppermint, Pine, Rose, Sage, Sandalwood, Spearmint, Spikenard, Spruce, Tangerine, Thyme, Valerian, Wintergreen and Ylang Ylang.*

Respect the fact that essential oils are derived from nature's botanicals and are said to be seventy times more concentrated than what is found in the original plant form. Be sure to do a skin patch test and dilute them before applying directly on the skin. It is recommended that you consult a person who has experience with essential oils to expand awareness of what these precious oils can do to nurture and energize your life.

The first step should be to study the characteristics and benefits each has to offer. A good way to do this is to select a new oil each week, dilute it and apply one or two drops on the pulse point inside your wrist to invigorate and refresh you throughout the day. You are the best judge as to how a fragrance will work ~ or not work ~ for you. As your knowledge increases, you will form a special relationship with certain oils that will elevate the quality of all your experiences.

> Note: The following tips and recipes are offered for your pleasure and not as treatment for any physical or mental illness or condition. Consult your physician before embarking on any new health practice.

## Essential Oil Tips & Recipes

As you experiment and expand your knowledge of essential oils and what they can do ~ you will be guided to the right oils at the right time to benefit your personal life. Begin your journey of discovery with these few basic tips and recipes.

### TIPS: *How to Use Essential Oils*

- Always skin test an essential oil before using it.
- Lift your spirits by diffusing your favorite oil into your surroundings.
- Add a few drops of lemon or peppermint to your washing machine or dishwasher.
- Keep lid tightly closed and store in amber glass containers away from heat and light.
- Never use essential oils while sitting directly in sunlight or using a tanning bed.
- Wait at least an hour to apply your oils after exercising or using a sauna or steam bath.
- Be careful to dilute essential oils when applying directly to the skin, with the exception of lavender and melaleuca oils.

### RECIPES: *How Many Drops to Add to Your Warm Bath Water*

- *Mood Uplifter* ~ 5 drops of rosewood, 5 drops of lavender and 5 drops of rose.
- *Colds:* 15 drops of Eucalyptus and Pine.
- *Chapped Skin:* 30 drops of Lavender.
- *Sore Muscles* ~ 5 drops of lavender, 4 drops of marjoram, 3 drops of peppermint, 2 drops of chamomile.
- *Tension Headaches:* 20 drops of lavender.
- *Relaxation* ~ 8 drops of lavender, 6 drops of orange, 4 drops of chamomile.
- *Romance* ~ 6 drops of jasmine, 3 drops of rose, 6 drops of ylang ylang.

I will be happy to assist you in discovering how the power of Mother Nature's essential oils will nurture your well being and add pleasure to your daily life.

May I offer this Cherokee blessing to each of you ~

> *"May the warm winds of heaven blow softly upon you, and may the Great Spirit make Sunrise in your heart."*

# MAYA ANGELOU

Hailed as one of the great voices of contemporary literature and remarkable Renaissance woman: Poet, Educator, Activist, Producer and Director, Ms. Angelou's influence reaches beyond the barriers of race, creed and color into the hearts of people everywhere.

Chosen by then President Elect William Jefferson Clinton as the Inaugural Poet, the nation watched and listened as Maya Angelou eloquently delivered the passionate and beautiful poem, *"On The Pulse of Morning."* It's message of beauty and equality — for those who believe it's there — is one for which we long. If we could harness its power, we could create a more loving world.

Random House has published ten best sellers by Ms. Angelou:

*I Know Why the Caged Bird Sings*
*Just Give Me a Cool Drink of Water 'Fore I Die*
*Gather Together in My Name*
*Oh Pray My Wings are Gonna Fit Me Well*
*Singin' and Swingin' and Getting Merry Like Christmas*
*And Still I Rise The Heart of a Woman*
*Shaker, Why Don't You Sing?*
*All God's Children Need Traveling Shoes*
*Now Sheba Sings the Song*
*I Shall Not Be Moved.*

# WE ARE MORE ALIKE
# THAN UNALIKE

*A*ll through history great ladies have left their mark on civilization. Women who have fought, struggled, and won over circumstances and seemingly over fate, itself. Such a woman is Maya Angelou. Someday, I knew I would meet her.

*There's magic in believing. It's potent stuff. It's a generator.*

*It would take some time and perseverance on my part, but it paid off when I got a SURPRISE call. Finally, this day in a posh hotel in Raleigh, N.C., I would have a chance to visit with Maya Angelou, one of my first and most influential heroines, an extraordinary individual, whose gifts to American culture are beyond measurement.*

*Excerpts from Publisher's Interview with internationally acclaimed poet-philosopher Mia Angelou:*

**Pat Sampson (PS): Ms. Angelou, you are so much of your own woman, would you share a childhood memory that helped mold your personality?**

**Maya Angelou (MA):** Well, I'm no complainer. When my grandmother was raising me in Stamps, Arkansas, she had a particular routine when people who were known to be whiners entered her store. Whenever she saw a known complainer coming, she would call me from what I was doing and say conspiratorially, "Sister, come inside. Come". Of course, I would obey.

My grandmother would ask the customer, "How are you doing today, Brother Thomas?" The person would reply, "Not so good today Sister Henderson. You see, it's this summer heat. I hate it. Oh, I hate it so much. It frazzles me up and frazzles me down. It's almost killing me." Then my grandmother would stand stoically, her arms folded, and mumble, "Uh-huh, uh-huh". She then would cut her eyes at me and make certain that I had heard the lamentation.

At another time a whiner would mewl, "I hate plowing. That packed down dirt ain't got no reasoning, and mules ain't got no good sense. It's killing me. My feet and my hands stay sore, and I get dirt in my eyes, and up my nose. I just can't stand it". My grandmother would say, "Uh-huh, uh-huh", and them look at me and nod.

As soon as the complainer was out of the store, my grandmother would call me to stand in front of her. Then she would say the same thing she had said at least a thousand times, it seemed to me.

"Sister, did you hear what Brother So-and-So or Sister Much-to-Do complained about? You heard that?" I would nod, Mamma would continue, "Sister, there were people all over the world that last night, poor and rich, and white and black, but they never wake again. Sister, those who expected to rise did not. Their beds became their cooling boards, and their blankets became their winding sheets. These dead folks would give anything, anything at all, for just five minutes of this weather or ten minutes of that plowing those people were grumbling about. So, you watch yourself about complaining Sister. What you're supposed to do is change it. If you can't change it, change the way you think about it. Don't complain."

It is said that persons have few teachable moments in their lives. Mamma seemed to have caught me at each one I had, between the ages of three and thirteen. Whining is not only graceless, but can be dangerous. It can alert a brute that a victim is in the neighborhood.

**PS: What's happening, that so much violence exists in our society?**
**MA:** Some years ago there was a conference called Facing Evil at the Institute of the Humanities in Salado, Texas. I was one of the participants in a group that included the psychologist, Rollo May, Sam Proctor, a pastor from New York, a Tai Chi master who has a temple in China and also teaches in this country, to mention a few. In front of an audience of about two hundred people, including Miss Barbara Jordan, we took a serious look at evil, its causes and manifestations, in our society and everywhere else. I spoke about a theory

of mine, which probably stems a great deal from reading Martin Luther early on, and also from everybody else I've read and loved and have been loved by. I believe it's likely that in the Universe there are two forces. One does not add value to these forces. One doesn't have to think of them as negative and positive, although, to describe them one could use these words. It may be that out of these forces in their pressure to take over, out of their struggle, comes life. Luther suggests that if aggressive force takes over, then the whole business will explode. It the passive force takes over, men will not woo women, and bridges will not be built. It is in that balance of the forces which is to be built upon. Having said all that as prologue it seems to me that the aggressive force is taking over.

**PS: Why is this the case?**
**MA:** Because too many of us have become inert, not just passive; because passive can become active in this theory; because too many of us have relinquished our charge to make peace and keep peace.

We have relinquished some of our autonomy because we are lazy and have given it to others, saying, "You take over". We don't want to use the energy to say, "This is right, and I will stand by it". It takes energy to be courageous, and courage is the most important of all the virtues. You can't be fair, or kind, or generous, or just, or merciful, or loving without courage. Not consistently. You can be that erratically. You know when it's convenient. So, I think that in our sloth, in our idleness, we have given some power to evil, and it burgeons. It's like algae and moss. It will take over the stream if the water is not moving. It will take over and slough it, and choke it. I think that is happening.

**PS: How can an individual find wisdom to help change things?**
**MA:** I do believe that all of our religious tracts, the Bible, the Torah, the Koran, the Bhagavad-Gita, give us the wisdom of the ages. Further, I think that we are obliged to study and recognize that one voice – ONE – one voice crying in the wilderness, one, can turn the whole thing around. Of course that takes great courage.

There is a wonderful Ethiopian song, written during the reign of Emperor Haile Selassie. He kept the poor very poor and the very rich disgustingly rich, and I mean that in the literal sense. So the song was written and sung by the poor people to make their lot in life easier to bear. It goes like this:

*(Here she sings the song in an unintelligible language, with a lot of animation and joy, translating as she goes along):*

"Don't tell me how beautiful you are, or how rich you are, or how young you are, or how healthy you are. If you do, you will force me to take you to the ends of the earth, where people much more fortunate than you have willingly jumped off. Don't think that the world holds you on top of it like a satisfied woman holds a lover. The world is doing what it does in the universe, and if it ever stops doing what it is doing, you'd slide right off."

*(She rolls her eyes amid raucous laughter).*

So, you see, too many of us act like its all about us. Not so. Not so!

**PS: So, what does an individual do to help change things?**
**MA:** Reach one — teach one. It's so glib, but so true. Each one — reach one.

**PS: I know how much you love children. Would you like to send them a message?**
**MA:** Among other things, every morning look in the mirror and say, GOD LOVES ME, and then work at having a cheerful heart. The Judeo Christian *Bible* says it. A cheerful heart is good medicine. It's so wonderful. Learn to laugh. Laugh not at anybody's expense, but laugh. Take life seriously, very seriously. It's serious business, but be willing to laugh at yourself. Don't be too ponderous. Forgive yourself your trespasses, and go on. I think that possibly what we all have to do is to forgive ourselves as quickly as possible. Further, its very important for young people to have a curiosity. Very.

So, sometimes they can wet their own curiosity by showing interest in anything. Someone says: I'll show you how to forge a piece of iron. Great! Show me. Teach me. I want to learn.

**PS: What advice would you give parents of young children today?**

**MA:** First, honor and cherish them, and read to them. Puzzles are wonderful. When the adult joins in with a child in trying to work a puzzle, or a word game, or charades, the child's intellect is engaged and cheer enters into it because it's fun.

I think if I were raising a young child today, I would indeed engage him or her in puzzles, in card games, and in parlor games. It seems on the face of it a very shallow and frivolous thing, but it isn't. It isn't at all. It engages their intellect. They get to laugh; they get to think; they get to wonder, to wonder in the large sense of the word; they can become amused. They can be taught, and they can teach themselves. That's what I would do.

**PS: What is the most important thing in life?**

**MA:** LOVE. By love I don't mean indulgence, and I don't mean sentimentality. I think love is that condition in the universe that holds the stars. I think it's that cohesive element which holds the molecules together. It's the DNA of life. That's it.

Literally the very structure of life itself is what I mean by love. It accepts that human beings are more alike than we are unalike. It accepts the differences and viva la difference, but the differences only heighten our similarities. It means taking responsibility for the time you take up and the space you occupy.

That's what I mean by love, and to be more willing to be inclusive as opposed to exclusive. That's what I mean by love. Accepting that my life is finite, and yet my life, my contribution through my life can be infinite. That's what I mean by love. Not being afraid of death. Not wanting it, but knowing it is part of life. That's what I mean by love.

*Time sped by quickly and too soon it was time to go. I would cherish the memory of this day as one of those rare occasions when a personality of that magnitude not only meets, but also exceeds expectations. It is crystal clear that although Maya Angelou is a friend of presidents and royalty, her LOVE for others is what makes her such a radiantly fulfilled human being.*

# DENNIS J. HOPKINS

**dennis j hopkins** was born and grew up in Nebraska. After graduating from the University of Nebraska with a major in Mathematics and a Minor in Psychology, his business career has included being an Actuary, an executive for a life insurance company, and finally a Financial Planner in Houston. Desiring a simpler and less complicated life in order to pursue his spiritual journey, he's now in the process of changing both his profession and place of residence.

Doing the thing he loves is the man's fulfillment. His poetry is an offering of the spirit and the heartbeat of the man. His sensitivity remains unspoiled and gentleness is the core of his strength. The words make their debut in his heart before they are released to the world. And when the world hears, it responds to the beat.

His poetry reaches out to the heart and soul, touching on basic human instincts, wants and needs, hopes and dreams, fears and regrets. Often his words act as a catalyst, encouraging others to examine their own past experiences, behavior patterns, and belief systems. The images he creates so beautifully illuminate the realization of personal choice and inspire the faith to follow one's own destiny to become the being of light inside us all.

**For more poetry by dennis j hopkins
visit his website at:
http://dennisjhopkins.com**

# THE GIFTS

Our gifts to others cover the entire spectrum
of so many different colors, hues, and shades
It might be saying, "I love you," to someone
when they need to hear that most of all
It might be smiling at a stranger
and expecting nothing at all in return
It might be not stepping on a spider
because its life has an important purpose too
It might be giving of yourself and time
when all you want to do is to be alone
And as important a lesson as gifting is to learn,
one must also be mindful of being able to receive
So accept the gifts our Father has given unto us,
to be responsible for the nurturing of our souls,
and to be eternally obligated to make progress
towards the very best that we can become
How wondrous and precious these gifts truly are,
to be able to mold a soul with our own hands
Oh, there are messengers who come into our lives,
reminding us of opportunities to learn our lessons
And life's experiences come to us each and everyday,
giving us ample reasons to grow and gain wisdom
But it is our own free will which gives us a choice
as to when and how we learn that which we need to know
So accept the gifts you are given and use them wisely,
as you would love for one of your gifts to be utilized
For when you learn to give and receive unconditionally,
you will discover something very wonderful indeed,
that the illumination you feel in your heart and soul
is a never-ending circle of love which binds us all together
within and without all that ever was, is, or will be

© dennis j hopkins

# CHAINS

Oh, how these chains do bind me,
far more than those ever imposed by others
For I have forged these links I bear
with my own heart, passion, and soul
And, does it really matter
that I had the best of intentions
during every event when I decided
to add more, rather than less, to my burden
I've worn them so very long now
that I almost considered them to be natural
And is it not amazing and troubling
what one imposes upon oneself
So, how does one begin
to unravel these numbing constraints
and move truly forward into the light
with a gentler set of self imposed bonds
Could it be as simple as looking
at each segment of one's own creation
and then deciding which ones are worthy
of being a part of whom we wish to become
Because after all , if one cannot allow
one's own ideals of oneself to come true,
is one deserving of assistance from above
in becoming the best that one can be
So, I have decided to begin the journey
of self discovery and the trusting of my inner voices,
which I have denied for far too long
in my quest for immediate gratification
And, I realize there will be some bumps in the night
and some unpleasant realizations
about whom I've allowed myself to become
in the here and now
But, if I'm ever to reach my goals,
do I not have to begin
with whom I've been, whom I am now,
and whom I wish to become

© dennis j hopkins

# SEABIRD

I remember the day that I fell down on the shore,
where I had so often gone
to visit with my dreams of what would be
But not this day, for I was too broken
to ever want to rise again
I just wanted to die quietly
and gain some kind of release
from those unrelenting torments

of my shattered hopes and dreams
I could even feel the numbness
begin to beckon me to sleep,
perhaps to dream again
Not that it mattered so much to me anymore
But then something caught my eye,
a darting movement down the shore
just a few feet away from where I lay
And in spite of my cold indifference,
I became entranced by what I saw
There was a little Seabird running back and forth in the surf,
dueling with the waves which were rushing in
and threatening to engulf it
The Seabird seemed so tiny and fragile
against these mighty fingers of the ocean,
but it never once failed to rush into harm's way
in a dedicated search for what it was seeking
Surprising myself, I began to admire
its courage and determination
while I silently began to root for it
I was never sure whether or not
it actually found what it was after,
but somewhere in this silent vigil
I found what was missing in me
As I finally rose to my knees
with tears of understanding
streaming down my cheeks,
I thanked God for sending this sign
of his love and compassion
to a pilgrim who had lost his sight,
perspective, and faith for a time

© dennis j hopkins

# GROWING

Sometimes it's just so hard and confusing
when you realize something is missing
and your life is not what you want it to be
And it's so difficult to have patience
while waiting for the answers to appear
for issues and questions you're not even sure of
These are the times when one seeks solitude,
for all too often you feel there really isn't anyone
whom you could talk to and who would understand
Fear also comes calling upon your mind
as you wonder if there is something wrong
with the basic nature of whom you are
Your heart and soul are sent reeling
into the darkness of despair and loneliness,
and tears come readily for no apparent reason
It's so easy for one to ignore and forget
that the reason we have these episodes
is to give us the opportunity to learn and grow
And, I hope you'll remember during such times
that I'm your friend and that I've been there too,
and I'll be there for you as you would for me
Let us remind each other that life is temporal
and that we are here to learn our lessons,
but also wondrously, that the soul is eternal
So there is simply all the time we will ever need
to grow and become that which we wish to be,
and we can comfort and nurture each other
while we're experiencing such troubling times
So let us be eternally thankful and appreciative
that we somehow found each other to share
our growing pains as well as our progress

© dennis j hopkins

# Thoughts Shape Your Destiny

### James Allen
You are today where your thoughts have brought you.
You will be tomorrow where your thoughts take you.

### Ralph Waldo Emerson
Life consists of what a man is thinking about all day.

### Euripides
Second thoughts are ever wiser.

### William A. Ward
Nothing limits achievements like small thinking.
Nothing expands possibilities like unleashed thinking.

### John Locke
The actions of men are the best interpreters of their thoughts.

### Henry David Thoreau
Each thought that is welcomed and recorded is a nest egg,
by the side of which more will be laid.

### Norman G. Shidle
We can't always control what happens to us.
But we can control what we think about what happens.
And what we are thinking is our life at any particular moment.

### Frank Crane
Our best friends and our worst enemies are our thoughts.
A thought can do us more good than a doctor or a banker
or a faithful friend. It can also do us more harm than a brick.

### Patrick Delany
Think all you speak, but speak not all you think.
Thoughts are your own; your words are so no more.

### Ralph Waldo Emerson
We do not yet trust the unknown powers of thought.
Whence came these tools, inventions, books, laws, parties, kingdoms?
Out of the invisible world, through a few brains.
The arts and institutions of men are created out of thought.
The powers that make the capitalist are metaphysical,
The force of method and force of will makes trade, and builds towns.

### John Burroughs
I still find each day too short for all the thoughts I want to think,
all the walks I want to take; all the books I want to read, and
all the friends I want to see. The longer I live, the more my mind
dwells upon the beauty and the wonder of the world.

# El Dorado

**Published in the *Commercial and Financial Chronicle*
December 10, 1932**

El Dorado, a country rich beyond all precedent in gold and jewels, lies at every man's door. Your bonanza lies under your feet. Your luck is already at hand. All is within; nothing is without; though it often appears that men and people by dumb luck or avarice or force or overreaching strike upon bonanzas and sail away in fair weather on the sea of prosperity... Man individually and collectively are entitled to life in all abundance. It is a most evident fact. Religion and philosophy assert it; history and science prove it. "That they might have life, and that they might have it more abundantly," is the law. What do you seek? Pay the price and take it away. There is no limit to the supply, but the more precious the thing you seek, the higher the price. For everything we obtain, we must barter the gold of our own spirits.

Where to find the gold of the All Powerful? One secures the gold of the spirit when he finds himself. When he finds himself, he finds freedom and all riches, achievement, and prosperity. High-sounding talk? No, it is the most palpable evidence of American history and biography, of all history. The concrete proof is apparent even in current events if we open our eyes. Nothing substantial, lasting, powerful, or moving was ever accomplished, nor can be, except by men and women who have discovered in themselves the gold of the spirit, which commands dominion, power, and accomplishment. Men and women who know themselves know at once that all material things and ideas have a spiritual counterpart or basis. They see it in money and in credit. The law of supply and demand is not to an awakened man – or woman – merely an economic principle operating in gravitation, in chemical affinities, in macrocosm, and in microcosm.

America has long been the greatest of El Dorados, the stage upon which the most numerous of self-found men and women worked their bonanzas and their miracles of thought to the enrichment of themselves and humankind at large. There is no exploitation, only a showering of gifts easily brought by free spirits and generously scattered on all hands according to the expressed law of bargain of the Original, Permanent Owner, and First Producer. To the self-found man or woman of action, all the money, credit, and capital goods one can use. . . Mackay, O'Brien, Hearst, Fair, and brave young Americans of 1849, found gold in themselves before they struck it rich in California. They had to. "If there is gold there," they told one another, "we'll get our share."

How great must have been the spiritual wealth of such a free-found man as James J. Hill, who built the Great Northern Road from nowhere to nowhere, in a wilderness where no one lives. His madness founded an empire. By spiritual force he turned forests and plains into a thousand El Dorados, and by the same force, commanded all the gold and credit needed for the markets of Amsterdam and London and enabled millions of Americans to discover for themselves great bonanzas in the cold Northwest.

Thomas A. Edison said a few years before he died, "Ideas come from space. This may seem astonishing and impossible to believe, but it is true. Ideas come from out of space." Surely, Edison should have known, for few men ever received or gave forth more ideas. Let each man seek the El Dorado within himself. Power is plentiful. The source is inexhaustible. As the Canonical Fathers of the church expressed it, that which is received is according to the measure of the recipient. It is not the power that is lacking, it is the will. When one finds oneself, the will becomes automatically set toward El Dorado.

By a full and powerful imagination anything can be brought into concrete form. The great physician, Paracelsus, said, "The human spirit is so great a thing that no man can express it. Could we rightly comprehend the mind of man, nothing would be impossible to us upon the earth. Through faith, the imagination is invigorated and completed, for it really happens that every doubt mars its perfection. Faith must strengthen the imagination, for faith established the will."

Faith is personal and individual. Salvation, any way you take it, is personal. Faith comes in the finding of one's self. This self-finding establishes a clear realization of one's identity with the eternal. Strong, self-assertive men build up this El Dorado of America. "Know thyself, thine own individual self", is everlasting the supreme command. Self-knowers always dwell in El Dorado. They drink from the fountain of youth and are at all times owners of all they wish to enjoy.

# Shelley L. Flynn

Shelley is currently studying for certification in natural therapies and shares living space with her son and two feline companions. Shelley's writing is a reflection of her own quest for enlightenment and self-discovery. She sees life as a spiritual learning experience, and as a glorious opportunity for each person to focus on their own inner beauty and light. nilla@nillavision.com

## CRYSTAL DREAMS

Such a wondrous dream I had ...
I found myself standing in a cavern of unknown size ...
I could see neither walls nor ceiling, but it felt as though
I was in an enclosed space of infinite proportions ...
at the center of this cavern there was a marble
pedestal which held a faceted crystal ...
This crystal shone with a soft inner illumination that
was the only visible source of light, and its beauty and
radiance fascinated me ... as I stood before it, I could
see that some facets were smooth, their colorful sparkle
clear and bright, yet other facets were still rough and
unfinished, their light somewhat murky and dim ...
it was obviously a "work in progress", not yet fully
polished yet breathtakingly beautiful even in its
incompleteness ...
I extended my hands toward it, afraid to touch it but
drawn to be as close as possible to the radiance it
offered ... so warm was the light, so soothing yet
uplifting at the same time, and the nearer I held my
hands to it, the more its illumination increased, as if
its inner light was being drawn to the surface because
of my wonder and awe ...
And on reflection (if I may be allowed such a pun),
I've come to realize that this beautifully faceted crystal
represents my own soul ... some facets are brighter than
others, while others have not yet been "polished" ... yet to
recognize the existence of the soul is the first step toward
enhancing the light that can and does shine from within
whom we are, and we have all of eternity to create whom
we wish to become ...

# THE GARDEN

Have you ever walked through the garden of your soul
   for the simple pleasure of self-illumination
Have you allowed yourself to notice each and every
   growing thing that makes you whom you are
Each has meaning and has contributed to your life,
   thereby influencing your soul's growth
The flowers might be the love you've shared,
   and the trees might symbolize the roots
   that help to stabilize your existence
Moss and ivy around the trees
   are the greening influences that
   keep us interested in our own growing
Even the weeds have their significance,
   for they are the neglected or undeveloped
   parts of our heart and soul
They represent the life lessons
   we have not yet learned or dealt with
Cool misting fountains give us rest and peace
   and a place of serenity in times of turmoil or strife
Your own garden might be laid out in neat patterns,
   or it might appear to be a tangled wilderness
It might be a combination of both
Whichever it happens to be,
   know that you and you alone
   are responsible for its growth and beauty
So when you take a walk through
   the garden of your soul
   look closely and see which parts call to you
   for they are the areas that might need care
And only you can cultivate and nurture
   the garden of your soul
   toward its full potential and growth

© Shelley L. Flynn

# EVERYBODY COLLECTS SOMETHING

Although I don't recall where or when I first heard
these words, from personal observation, I've
found it to be true ... in fact, most people seem
to collect more than just one something ...
It is a constant fascination to me, the combination
of things people collect ... the person who collects
ceramic figurines might have shelves of empty
boxes, and someone who collects crystal might
have stacks of little plastic containers ...
I'll admit that boxes of varying sizes come in handy
at Christmas time, and plastic containers are
great for leftovers, but I also wonder sometimes
just how many is 'enough' ...
It's so much more than mere possessions,
though ... each of us collects moments of
happiness and joy ... memories of first love,
of children born, friends ... the things so
special to us .... but we also have a tendency
to collect less positive things ... old hurts,
grudges, anger ... some would say this is
simply human nature, but why must it be
this way ...
I think about beauty ... the sparkling crystal,
or the delicate figurines ... the loveliness that
makes us catch our breath with wonder ... and
the empty boxes and containers that can be
and are useful to a point but can so easily
accumulate to little more than clutter ...
Everyone collects something ... we each
collect that which is valuable to us, that
which we hold dear ... and how much more
peaceful the world would be if people 'let go'
of the inner clutter of hatred, anger, and
prejudice, choosing instead to 'collect'
and enhance the positive, bright aspects
of their own inner light ...

© Shelley L. Flynn

# SEARCHING FOR FREEDOM

Freedom of the soul is the
release of extra baggage,
the shedding of the chains we all carry
as we release each link of fear, jealousy,
resentment, grudges, and anger,
while holding on to the things
which are truly important
It is freedom to be responsible to and for
our own thoughts, words, and actions,
without seeking anyone or anything to blame
for the pitfalls that occur in every life
It is the freedom to put yourself first
without apology or guilt,
to pursue the wants, needs, and lessons
that are necessary in order to become the
best of whom we are capable of being
All this isn't easy, although it
seems as if it should be,
but there are times when it's
challenging or downright difficult
Freedom can bring feelings of separation,
even from family members who have grown
used to whom we've always been to them,
or whom they thought we were
Freedom can bring feelings
of alienation from the people
we encounter every day,
since the things which mean
so much to them no longer
hold us enthralled
Money, material possessions,
power, and control over others
are seen as transitory trappings
unimportant and not worth acquiring
I cherish the freedom
I've found in this lifetime,
and I know that one day
I will indeed be completely free

© Shelley L Flynn

# SONNY CARROLL

**Sonny Carroll** is a sales and marketing professional who specializes in helping companies to develop highly effective sales organizations. Her personal passion and interests include, writing and speaking about women's issues including money, personal power and relationships, whereby she endeavors to inspire, educate and motivate women to take control of their lives and realize their dreams. You can find more of Sonny's work on her website, www.waketolife.com.

# Self-Love

It was a Saturday morning ~ house cleaning day. Absently, I reached for a can of Ajax beneath the bathroom sink and caught a glimpse of myself in the mirror. For a second, I was taken aback. The way you are when you run across an old acquaintance and try to place the face.

*"You,"* I heard myself say, *"It's you. I hadn't noticed you standing there all this time."*

I looked at myself. My age was beginning to show. I looked carefully at the contours of my face, my nose, and the tiny beauty mark on the side of my mouth. No judgments… just recognition. Then I looked deep into my eyes, my beautiful brown eyes.

I felt myself gazing the way you do when upon first meeting, you seem to recognize the soul of another. *"Hello."* I heard myself whisper. *"Oh my God, I've never noticed you standing there. Standing and waiting for me to recognize you. All this time it's been you there beside me."* You said nothing, but in your eyes, I saw it all.

You had walked every step of the way with me. You picked me up when I fell. When others walked away, you stayed. And every time I thought I couldn't go on you gave me the strength and showed me the way. I never acknowledged you. I never championed you. I never took care of you. I never acknowledged your goodness, your gifts or your strength. I had love for everyone else but none for you. "Forgive me." I heard myself cry. "I never meant to hurt you. You… the one that has always been there for me. Let me love and honor you. I promise never to betray you again." You said nothing, but in your eyes, I saw a smile.

234

There comes a time in your life when you finally get it.... When in the midst of all your fears and insanity you stop dead in your tracks and somewhere the voice inside your head cries out - **enough!** Enough fighting and crying or struggling to hold on. And, like a child quieting down after a blind tantrum, your sobs begin to subside, you shudder once or twice, you blink back your tears and through a mantle of wet lashes you begin to look at the world from a new perspective. **This is your awakening**.

You realize that it is time to stop hoping and waiting for something, or someone, to change or for happiness, safety and security to come galloping over the next horizon. You come to terms with the fact that there aren't always fairytale endings (or beginnings for that matter) and that any guarantee of "happily ever after" must begin with you. Then a sense of serenity is born of acceptance.

You begin making your way through the "reality of today" rather than holding out for the "promise of tomorrow." You realize that much of who you are, and the way you navigate through life is, in great part, a result of all the social conditioning you've received over the course of a lifetime. And you begin to sift through all the nonsense you were taught ~ how you should look and what you should weigh ~ what you should wear and where you should shop ~ where you should live or what type of car you should drive ~ who you should sleep with and how you should behave ~ who you should marry and why you should stay ~ the importance of having children ~ or what you owe your family.

You accept that you are not perfect and not everyone will love, appreciate or approve of who or what you are... and that's OK... *they are entitled to their own views and opinions.* You will never be a size 5 or a "perfect 10" ~ *or a perfect human being for that matter.* So you stop competing with the image inside your head or agonizing over how you compare. You promise yourself the same unconditional love and support you give so freely to others. Then a sense of confidence is born of self-approval.

You begin to love and to care for yourself. You stop engaging in self-destructive behaviors including participating in dysfunctional relationships. You begin eating a balanced diet, drinking more water and exercising. And because you've learned that fatigue drains the spirit and creates doubt and fear, you give yourself permission to rest. And just as food is fuel for the body, laughter is fuel for the spirit and so you make it a point to create time for play.

*You give thanks for simple blessings ~ things that millions of people upon the face of the earth can only dream about ~ a full refrigerator, clean running water, a soft warm bed and ~ the freedom to pursue your own dreams.*

You learn about love and relationships, how to love, how much to give in love, when to stop giving and when to walk away. And you allow only the hands of a lover who truly loves and respects you to glorify you with his touch. You learn that people don't always say what they mean or mean what they say, intentionally or un-intentionally, and that not everyone will always come through for you. Interestingly enough, it's not always about *you*. So, you stop lashing out or looking to place blame. You learn to keep your ego in check by acknowledging and then redirecting the destructive emotions it spawns; anger, jealousy and resentment.

You learn to admit when you are wrong and to forgive people for their own human frailties. You learn to build bridges instead of walls and about the healing power of love ~ a kind word, a warm smile or a friendly gesture. And, at the same time, you eliminate hurtful relationships. You stop working so hard at smoothing things over and setting your needs aside. You learn the importance of communicating your needs with confidence and grace. You distinguish between guilt, and responsibility and the importance of setting boundaries and saying *NO*. You acknowledge that you don't know all the answers, it's not your job to save the world, and sometimes you just need to *let go*.

You see people as they really are and not as you would want them to be. You are careful not to project your neediness or insecurities onto a relationship. People grow and change and not everyone can always love you the way you would want them to. So you stop appraising your worth by the measure of love you are given.

Suddenly, you realize that it's wrong to demand that someone live their life or sacrifice their dreams just to serve your needs, ease your insecurities, or meet *"your"* standards and expectations. You learn that the only love worth giving and receiving is the love that is given freely without conditions or limitations. You learn about unconditional love. You stop trying to control people, situations and outcomes. You know "alone" does not mean "lonely" and discover the joy of spending time "with yourself" and "on yourself." You discover the greatest and most fulfilling love you will ever know. Self Love. Through understanding your heart heals; and now all new things are possible.

Moving along, you begin to avoid toxic people and conversations. You stop wasting time and energy rehashing your life with family and friends. Talk doesn't change things and unrequited wishes only serves to keep you trapped in the past. So, you stop lamenting over what could or should have been and make a decision to leave the past behind. You begin to invest your time and energy to affect positive change. You take a personal inventory of all your strengths and weaknesses and the areas you need to improve in order to move ahead. You set goals and map out a plan of action to see things through.

Life isn't always fair and you don't always get what you think you deserve ~ so you stop personalizing every loss or disappointment. You accept that sometimes bad things happen to good people and that these things are not an act of God...but merely a random act of fate. You make it a point to keep smiling, keep trusting, and staying open to every wonderful opportunity and exciting possibility.

Then you hang a wind chime outside your window to remind yourself what beauty there is in Simplicity.

Finally, with courage in your heart and with God by your side you take a stand, you *fake* a deep breath and you begin to design the life you want to live as best as you can.

# Tom Walsh

**Tom Walsh** is a student of life who lives with his wife, Terry, and stepchildren in Keene, New Hampshire. Tom previously served as an intelligence analyst in the U.S. Army. Presently he is a college teacher at Landmark College in Putney, VT, a small college that specializes in teaching students with Learning Disorders.

His first novel, *(If I should Die) Before I Wake*, was recently published by *PublishAmerica*.

His "modest contribution to the world" is *livinglife-fully.com*. *Living Life Fully* is a labor of love to share with others who desire a more fulfilling life.

# You're a Beautiful Person

I wish that I could tell every person that I meet that he or she is a beautiful person — and have them believe it. I wish I could look them in the eyes and tell them of their beauty and have them accept the words for what they truly are — the truth, plain and simple.

You know what I mean, don't you? You and I both know that most people will deny their beauty, expressing what they feel is modesty or humility. It's easier for us to be told that we're talented or intelligent — our own beauty is something that we don't want to face.

You could help me to convince people of their innate beauty. You could agree with me in an effort to reinforce the message. You could give a few specifics to illustrate just what we're talking about when we say the person is beautiful. You could reassure the person that I'm not saying it to flatter or to try to win the person over or get something out of the person, but just trying to express in words the beauty I see when I look into that person's eyes and see the human being there, the person who gets happy and hurt and who laughs and who cries.

You can help me by reminding the person that beauty isn't about comparing ourselves with others, but about the part of us that shines when we love others and love life. It's not all physical and it's not all spiritual, but a tender combination of all that we are.

And when that person says, "No, not me," you could argue the point and ask him or her not to talk down about him or herself, to admit to the beauty that's there, to accept it, to thrive in it. Because you know just as well as I do that this person can hurt his or her own self-image and feelings by denying the beauty.

So I ask you: Please help me to convince people of their own beauty. Will you do that? Thank you.And we will start right here, with you: You are a beautiful person. The rest is up to you.

# Thoughts for Beautiful People

### Max Ehrmann
You are a child of the Universe, no less than the moon and the stars;
you have a right to be here. And whether or not it is clear to you,
no doubt the Universe is unfolding as it should.

### Ralph Waldo Emerson
Though we travel the world over to find the beautiful,
We must carry it with us or we will find it not.

### Washington Irving
Enthusiasts soon understand each other.

### — Anonymous
Some people weave burlap into the fabric of our lives, and some
weave gold thread. Both contribute to make the whole
picture beautiful and unique.

### Ernest Renan
Man makes holy what he believes, as he makes beautiful what he loves.

### George Eliot
It seems to me we can never give up longing and wishing
to be thoroughly alive.There are certain things we must feel to be
beautiful and good, and we must hunger after them.

### Johnann Wolfgang von Goethe
Every day look at a beautiful picture, read a beautiful poem,
listen to beautiful music, and, if possible, say some beautiful thing.

### Ralph Waldo Emerson
It is one of the most beautiful compensations of life, that no man can
sincerely try to help another without helping himself.

### Elizabeth Kubler-Ross
We are not powerless specks of dust drifting around in the wind,
blown by random destiny. We are, each of us, like beautiful
snowflakes unique, and born for a specific reason and purpose.

### Jerome P. Fleishman
Sure! Your Heart's Desire will come true some day. But you must trust
and, trusting, you must wait.You've but to vision to clear the brighter
way, and see what isn't written on the slate.You must *believe* that
happier, bigger things are coming toward you through the trying year.
Your ears must hear the rustle of the wings of God's glad messengers,
so dry your tears! Our trials are tests; our sorrows pave the way for a
fuller life when we have earned it so. Give rein to *faith* and hail the
brighter day, and you shall come at last real joy to know!

# The Dream Continues ....

**Pat Sampson**
**Founder & Publisher**

Pat Sampson's positive philosophy of life is rooted in the good fortune of finding employment — many moons ago — as an assistant to successful business and sales executives. From watching them she began to understand that to do well, you must first think well; and it all starts with believing in yourself. The office was a gold mine of positive people and positive thinking material. *Think and Grow Rich* was required reading; positive thinking books, tapes and seminars became part of daily life.

Finding herself the sole support of two little girls, she entered the world of sales. Pat's first year with one of the nation's leading community developers and with no previous sales experience, she ranked first in a four-thousand-strong sales force. After yearly achieving the company's highest honors, she sought new challenges in the competitive field of life insurance. Within six months she became the first woman in the Franklin Life Insurance Company's ninety-six year history, admitted to the exclusive Four Honor Club. Lauded as one of our nation's leading salespeople and as the subject of numerous media interviews and newspaper articles, Pat began sharing her story to encourage others facing their own challenges. At the height of her career she left financial rewards behind to write her first book, *A Star to Steer By*, which would be featured as Editor's Choice in *Success, Unlimited*.

Pat never looked back. A burning desire to create a venue for recognizing positive people resulted in publishing *Dreaming and Winning in America*, an inspirational collection of philosophies of ninety-five extraordinary Americans; and *Positive News, a Good News Tabloid*. Letters from people yearning for positive news poured in; and messages of encouragement from her heroes, W. Clement Stone and Dr. Norman Peale, cemented her commitment to a dream that would never go away. The dream continues to connect positive people everywhere.

"Join us! Together we light the way to a brighter tomorrow!"